59 Authentic Turn-of-the-Century Fashion Patterns

Kristina Harris

DOVER PUBLICATIONS, INC.
NEW YORK

The diagrams on page iv are taken from the author's *Peterson's Patterns for Civil War Era Ladies*, published by Pioneer Printwork, Springfield, Oregon, 1994, and are used with her permission.

Copyright

Published in Canada by General Publishing Company, Ltd., 30 Lesmill Road, Don Mills, Toronto, Ontario.

Published in the United Kingdom by Constable and Company, Ltd., 3 The Lanchesters, 162–164 Fulham Palace Road, London W6 9ER.

Bibliographical Note

59 Authentic Turn-of-the-Century Fashion Patterns, first published by Dover Publications, Inc., in 1994, is a selection of patterns from the following issues of *The Voice of Fashion*:

Vol. V, No. 18, Fall 1890; Vol. V, No. 19, Winter 1890–91; and Vol. V, No. 20, Spring 1891—all published by Goldsberry, Doran & Nelson, Chicago, Illinois.

Vol. VII, No. 28, Spring 1893; Vol. VIII, No. 29, Summer 1893; Vol. VIII, No. 32, Spring 1894; Vol. IX, No. 36, Spring 1895; and Vol. X, No. 39, Winter 1896—all published by Goldsberry & Doran, Chicago, Illinois.

Library of Congress Cataloging-in-Publication Data

Harris, Kristina.
    59 authentic turn-of-the century fashion patterns / Kristina Harris.
       p.   cm.
    Selection of patterns from various 1890's issues of the Voice of fashion.
    ISBN 0-486-28357-7 (pbk.)
    1. Dressmaking—Patterns. 2. Costume—United States—History—19th century.
3. Voice of fashion. I. Voice of fashion. II. Title. III. Title: Authentic turn-of-the century fashion patterns.
TT520.H277   1994
646.4'78—dc20   94-38091
                                                              CIP

Manufactured in the United States of America
Dover Publications, Inc., 31 East 2nd Street, Mineola, N.Y. 11501

INTRODUCTION

It is a common belief that ladies throughout the nineteenth century sewed all or most garments for themselves and their families; however, truth be told, most women of the middle and upper classes sewed far less prolifically—often making only undergarments and a few accessories. This was due, in part, to the lack of sewing patterns available. Although many fashion magazines from as early as the 1850s regularly included patterns and diagrams, these were difficult to use without some in-depth training in dressmaking. By the 1860s, Butterick was offering patterns as we know them today, but these, though within the grasp of many home sewers, were produced for only a few select garments.

Professional dressmakers, on the other hand, were usually trained and had at their disposal not only the patterns and diagrams readily available to the public, but also a myriad of patterns produced specifically for their trade.

The scaled patterns reprinted here, originally published in a quarterly magazine called *The Voice of Fashion*, were among the dressmaker's patterns offered in the 1890s.

With each issue of *The Voice of Fashion* came a poster depicting every garment in the magazine. These posters were put on display for clients to choose garments from. Once a client decided which garment she wanted, the dressmaker or her assistant (called a "cutter") would enlarge the scaled pattern onto either heavy paper or cardboard or directly onto fabric.

Possibly, these were the last patterns of their kind. Though dressmaker's patterns had thrived since the late eighteenth century, they would quickly be made obsolete by a rash of full-size paper patterns that would take over in the early 1900s. Though *The Voice of Fashion* would continue to be published well into the twentieth century, its slant would change—no longer would professional dressmakers be the publisher's target market. The home sewer would become the target market for the new century.

Today, these patterns remain as a testament of fashion—not the fashions pictured in fashion magazines and worn only by a select group of society, but the fashions worn by "everyday" people of the middle and upper classes. They are a means of documenting existing period garments, as well as accurately recreating fashions of the past.

HOW TO USE THE PATTERNS

The patterns given in this book are scaled. There are a number of different ways to enlarge them. For either of the two methods described here, you will need a pencil, a ruler, transparent tape and a roll of wrapping or shelf paper.

If all the patterns for a particular garment piece (such as the bodice) are in the same scale, the patterns can be enlarged by the grid method. An easy way to check whether they are in the same scale is to measure the line running along the right-hand side of the pattern. Divide this measurement into the number given at the bottom of the line. If the patterns are in the same scale, your results should be roughly the same for each piece. If the pattern pieces are to more than one scale or size, be sure to read the instructions for "The Grading Method."

The Grid Method

Begin with a major body measurement such as the waist. Next, add an appropriate amount of wearing ease (for most waistlines of this period, about ½″ is appropriate). Now, in order to figure your scale, compare this total measurement with the corresponding measurement on the scaled pattern; be sure to take seam allowances and pattern pieces that represent ½ or less of the garment into consideration. If, for example, the intended wearer has a 23½″ waist, plus ½″ for wearing ease, and the scaled pattern's waist measurement is 2″, the proper scale to use would be 1″/12″. In other words, every inch on the scaled pattern would equal 12″ on the full-size pattern.

Next, draw a grid on top of the scaled pattern (in this example, a 1″ grid), and then draw a grid on the shelf paper (in this example, a 12″ grid).

Now, transfer the lines of the scaled pattern onto the shelf paper, square by square. Whenever necessary, tape the shelf paper together to make it large enough for a full-size pattern.

The Grading Method

When garments illustrated show pattern pieces given in more than one scale, you should use the grading method. Notice that each pattern includes sets of numbers running along all pattern lines. The numbers running along the right-hand edge of the pattern indicate length measurements; the other numbers indicate the width. Draw the pattern lines onto your paper, following all measurements carefully. It may be helpful to draw a 1″ grid onto the paper before transferring pattern lines onto it, but it is not necessary. Where curves are shown, you may draw them freehand or with the aid of a French curve (available at dressmaking stores).

Once you have carefully drawn out each pattern piece according to the measurements given, you have created a "standard size" sloper for the garment. This, by modern standards, is quite small and will need to be graded to fit the modern figure. If you are unfamiliar with the practice of grading patterns, follow the instructions given below or consult a dressmaking book at your local library.

To Adjust Width: Changes will almost certainly need to be made in the width of your pattern. To determine how much change is necessary, subtract your actual measurements (including wearing ease and seam allowances) from the corresponding pattern measurements. For example, if your waist measurement is 25½″ and the pattern measurement is 19″, you need to enlarge your pattern by 6½″ in the waist area. Now, divide the amount you must enlarge the pattern (in our example 6½″) by the number of bodice pattern pieces (for our example, say 4). This will tell you how much to enlarge each pattern piece (in our example, 1⅝″). Slash the pattern pieces as illustrated in *Fig. 1*, and spread in a triangular fashion. Place a piece of paper behind the slashed section and tape it into place.

To take in the pattern, make a tuck in the pattern as shown in *Fig. 1* and redraw the cutting and seam lines.

To Adjust Length: If your garment needs adjustment in length, either fold it (if too long) or slash and spread it (if too short) *(Fig. 2)*.

Remember:

• In most cases, allowances for closures (hooks and eyes, buttons, plackets) and facings are not included on the pattern and must be added before cutting out the pattern in fabric.

• Carefully label all pattern pieces and transfer any construction markings to the full-size pattern.

• If a corset and other undergarments are to be worn, the body measurements should be taken in these undergarments.

• It may be necessary to use different scales for different parts of each garment even if the pattern pieces for each part are in the same scale. For instance, the bodice may require a larger scale than the skirt, especially if a corset will not be worn beneath the finished garment.

• The length of most skirt patterns is not proportional. Regulate the length of skirts by personal length measurements.

• Always remember to add wearing ease to your body measurements before figuring the scale on which to enlarge your pattern. If you make your pattern to your exact measurements, the resulting garment will be skin tight, and will probably rip with every movement. Ease must be added to make clothes fit comfortably. The typical 1890s waistline had about ½″ to 1″ ease, and the average snug-fitting bustline had about 2½″ of ease.

• Because there is no "standard" body, testing and perfecting the pattern in muslin before cutting out the fashion fabric is advised.

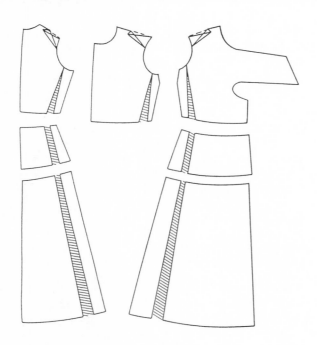

Fig. 1. To adjust width.

Fig. 2. To adjust length.

TO TAKE MEASURES. Great care should be taken in getting measures. (See illustration below.)

TAKE BUST MEASURE with the tape measure straight around the largest part of the bust, as shown below, high up under the arms; take a snug, close measure neither too tight nor too loose.

TAKE MEASURE AROUND THE WAIST as tight as the dress is to be worn.

TAKE LENGTH OF WAIST from the large joint where neck and body join, down to the waist. Care must be taken to get this measure.

SLEEVE MEASURE is taken from the center of back to wrist joint, with arm raised and elbow bent.

IN CUTTING a garment look carefully at the drafts being copied; use numbers and curves as shown in draft.

THE ARROWS are used for two purposes— one to show which way to turn the curve, the other the number of points to be connected with the curve.

THE CURVE should always be turned with the largest part in the direction in which the arrow points.

When the arrow is placed *between* two lines it shows that only two points are to be connected.

When the arrow is placed upon a *cross line* it shows that three points must be connected with the curve, that the point by the arrow is the middle one, and the points nearest on each side must be connected with the curve at the same time with larger part of the curve turned in the direction the arrow points.

The letter A in corner of draft is the starting point in making draft.

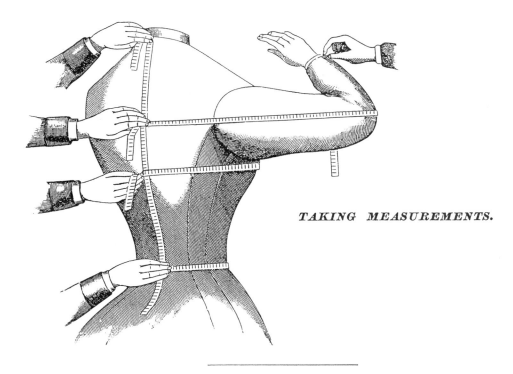

TAKING MEASUREMENTS.

DIRECTIONS FOR BASTING.

FIRST:—Smooth, even tracing is very necessary. Place the pattern smooth on lining crosswise. Trace each line carefully. Cut out the lining same as pattern. Place the lining straight on the goods, the nap, if any, running down. Pin the lining at the waist line. Full the lining (from ¼ to ½ inch) each side of the waist line, from 1½ inches below the waist line to 2½ inches above, the greatest fullness coming at the waist line; this shortens the lining, but when boned it will be stretched to place. Leave the lining easy each way, from top of darts to shoulders, and one-fourth of an inch full at center of shoulder line. Never backstitch in basting or draw the thread tight.

In joining the different parts together, care must be taken, as smooth, even basting is necessary. Pass the needle exactly through the traced seam lines on both sides of the seam, as many garments are ruined by careless basting.

In joining the back and side-back, hold the side-back to you, thus you will baste one up and the other down. It is a good idea to pin these pieces before basting. If the shoulder blades are prominent, hold the back piece a little full where the shoulder blades strike to within 1½ inches of arms-eye. In basting the shoulders, hold the back to you. Baste evenly for one inch, then stretch the front shoulder to match the back, for the back is always cut longer.

LADIES' COSTUME.

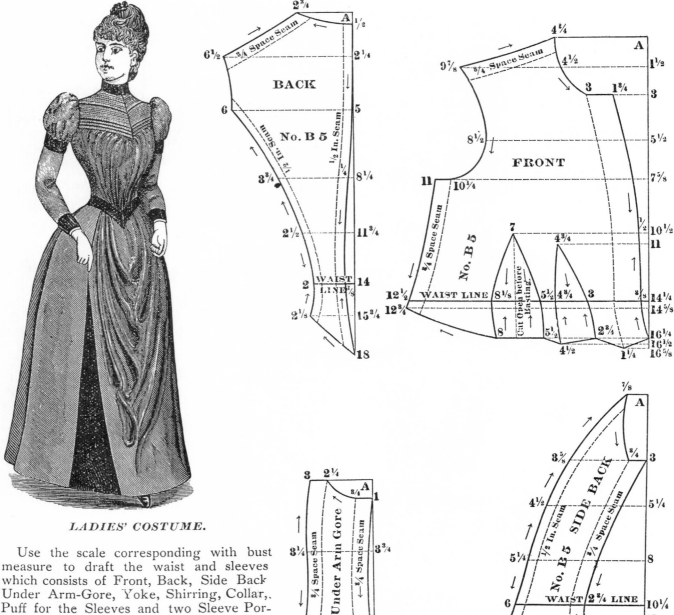

LADIES' COSTUME.

Use the scale corresponding with bust measure to draft the waist and sleeves which consists of Front, Back, Side Back Under Arm-Gore, Yoke, Shirring, Collar,. Puff for the Sleeves and two Sleeve Portions.

Gather the portions for the full front at the top and sew to the yoke. Lay the pleats at the bottom according to the notches; join to the under front at the under arm and shoulder seams; close in front with hooks and eyes.

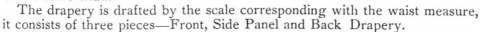

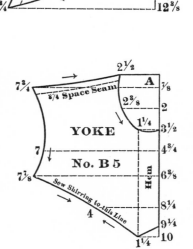

The back is plain, but may be made with a yoke same as the front, if desired; finish the bottom with a band of ribbon or velvet, two or three inches wide; finish in the back with loops and long ends of the same, gather the top of the puff and sew in with the sleeve; gather the bottom and finish with a band of velvet or ribbon; finish the sleeve at the hand with one or more bands of the same width.

The drapery is drafted by the scale corresponding with the waist measure, it consists of three pieces—Front, Side Panel and Back Drapery.

Lay the pleats according to the notches; the back is laid in two triple box pleats; make it as long as the skirt.

The diagrams for the skirt are given on page 5, it is drafted by the scale corresponding with the waist measure, is in three pieces—Front, Back and Side Gore. Regulate the length by the tape measure.

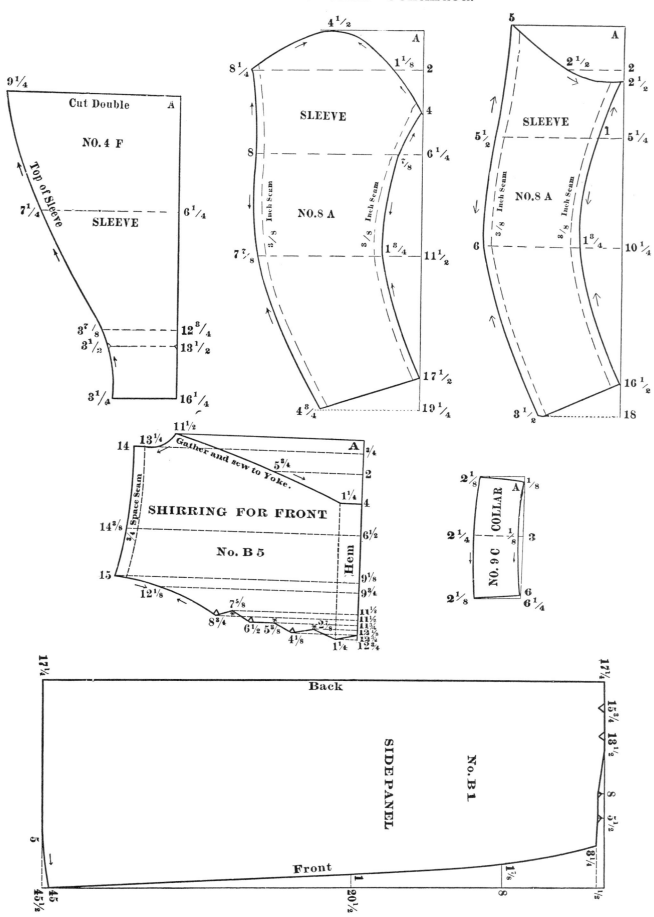

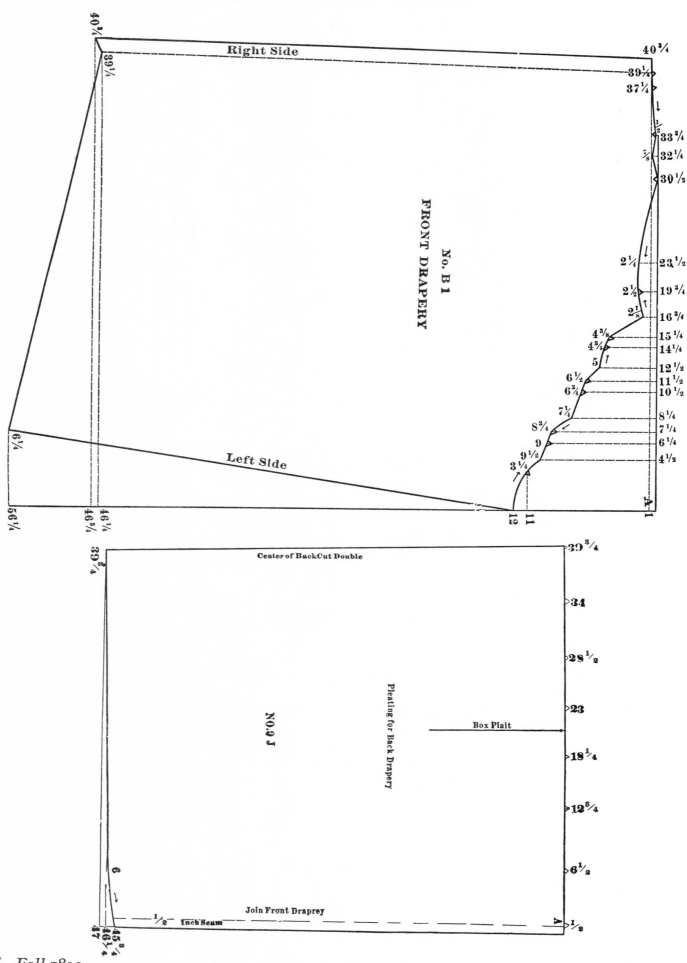

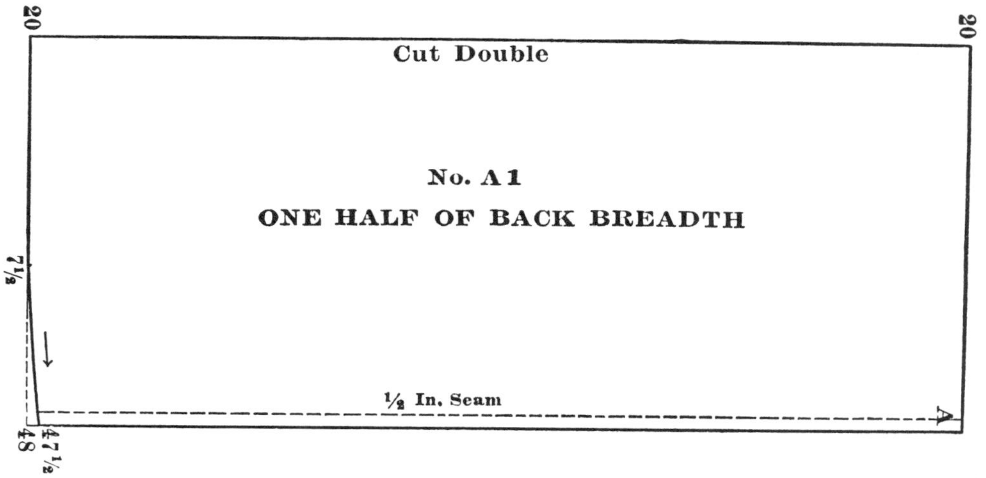
Cut Double
No. A 1
ONE HALF OF BACK BREADTH
½ In. Seam
20
20
7½
48
47½
A

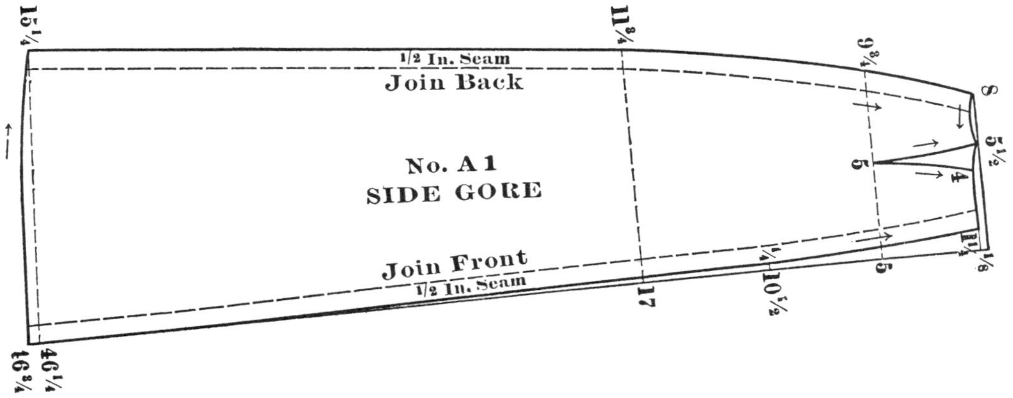
½ In. Seam
Join Back
No. A 1
SIDE GORE
Join Front
½ In. Seam
15¼
11¾
9¾
8
5½
5
4
5
17
10½
46¼
46¾

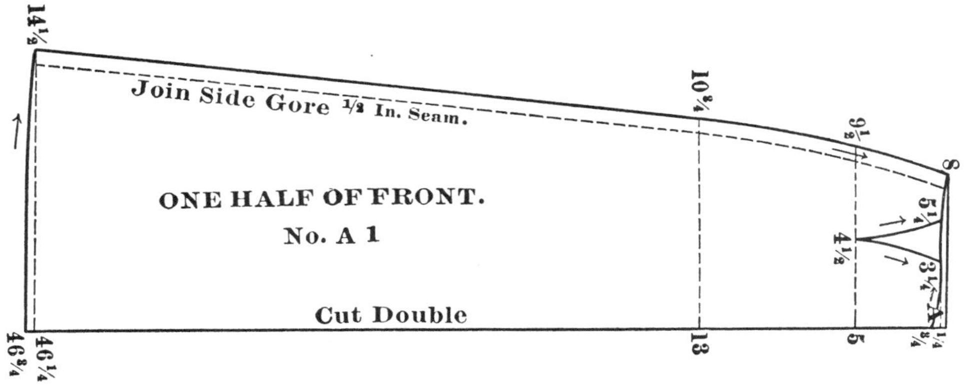
Join Side Gore ½ In. Seam.
ONE HALF OF FRONT.
No. A 1
Cut Double
14½
10¾
9½
8
5¼
4½
3¼
13
5
46¼
46¾

CHILD'S BLOUSE COSTUME.

CHILD'S BLOUSE COSTUME.

Use the scale corresponding with the bust measure to draft the waist and sleeves. It consists of nine pieces.

The blouse consists of front and back yokes, shirring for front and back, cuff, and three sleeve portions. Gather the front and back portions, and sew to the yoke: also gather the lower edge and sew to under waist. If made to wear during the warm season, omit the under waist; simply gather and sew to the skirt; bind the seams underneath to keep it in place. Gather the full sleeve at the top and bottom, and baste on the tight sleeve at the top and bottom.

The skirt is drafted by the waist measure. Regulate the length by the tape measure.

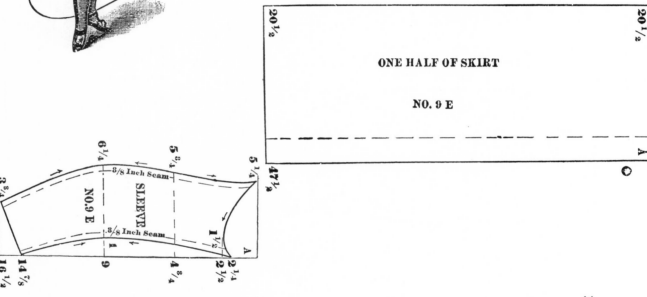

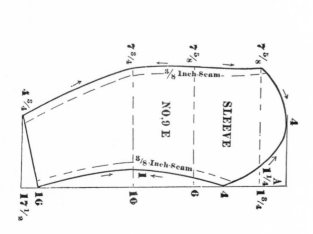

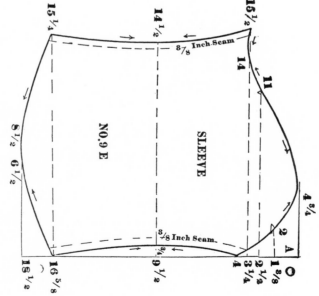

CHILD'S BLOUSE COSTUME—Continued.

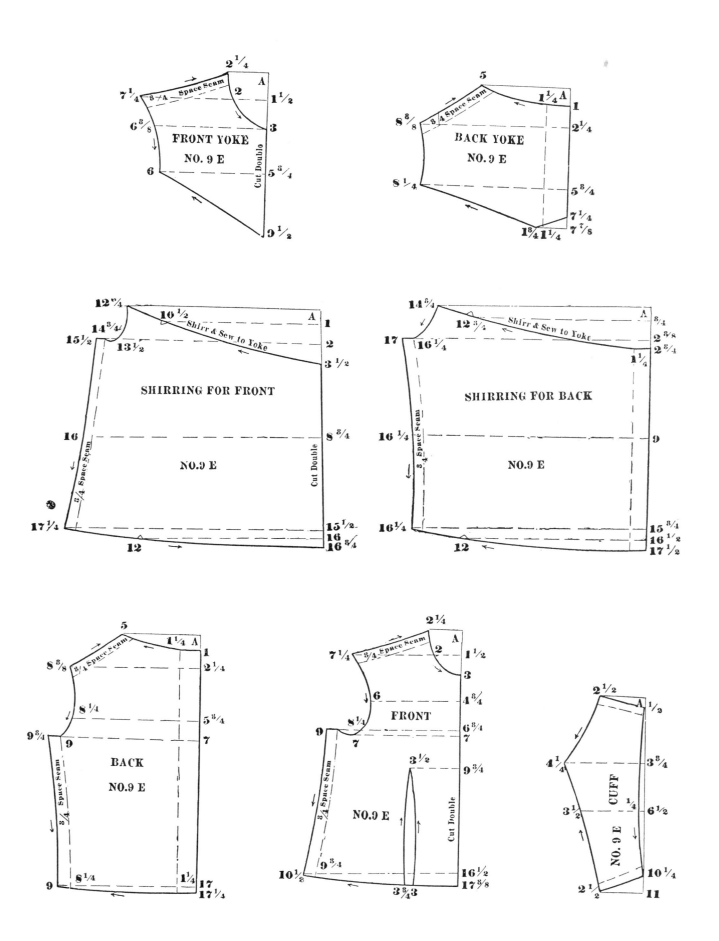

LADIES' WRAP.

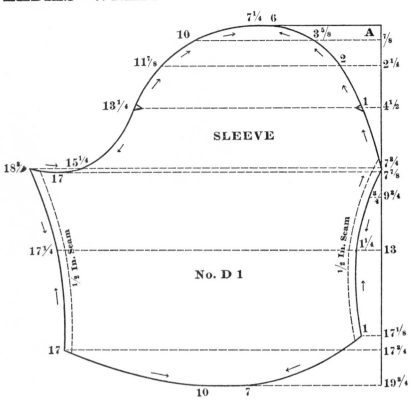

LADIES' WRAP.

Use the scale corresponding with the bust measure to draft the entire costume, which consists of Front, Back, Side-Back, Sleeve, Cuff, Belt, and four Collar pieces. Lay pleats in the back and front according to the notches, turn the pleats toward the center, stitch each pleat down as far as the notches; press carefully. Sew the belt in the under-arm dart. Gather the sleeve at the top between the notches, and sew in the arms eye. Gather at the bottom and sew on the cuff. It would be better to make a tight lining. Cut from any of the tight sleeve patterns.

The three collars, or capes, are faced with silk.

This makes a very stylish looking garment, as well as comfortable.

Regulate the length by the tape measure.

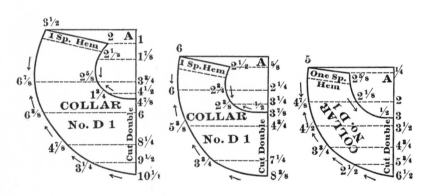

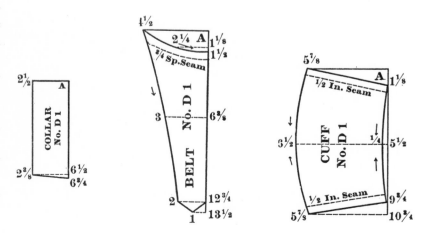

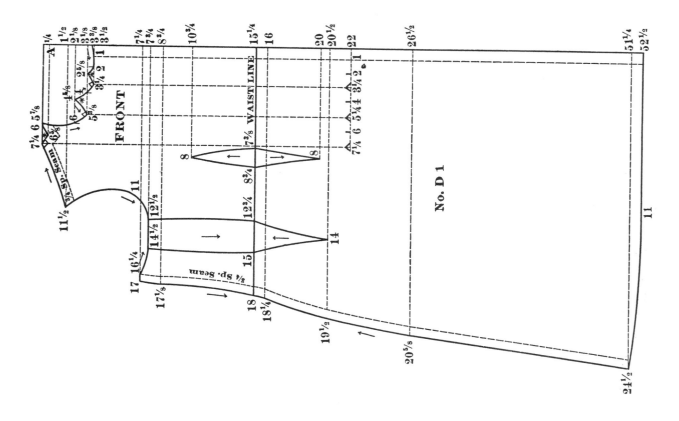

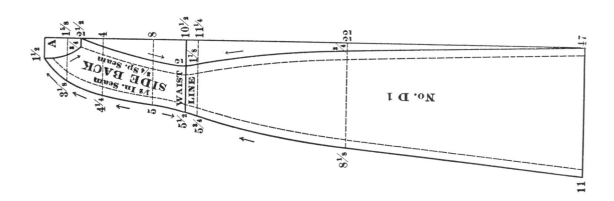

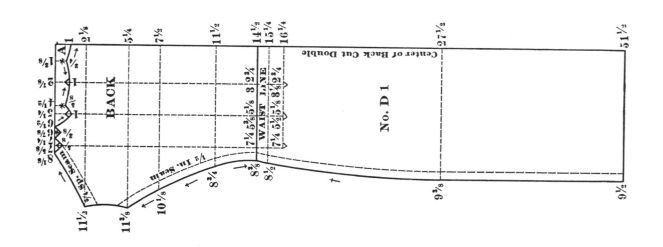

CHILD'S STREET COSTUME.

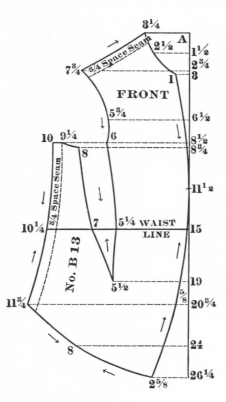

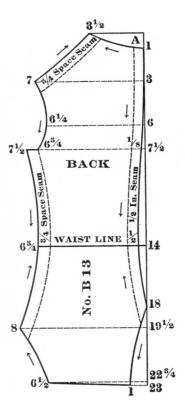

CHILD'S STREET COSTUME.

Use the scale corresponding with the bust measure to draft the jacket, blouse, waist, and also the under-waist.

The jacket consists of five pieces: Front, Back, Collar, and two Sleeve portions. Finish the bottom of this with a very fine silk cord.

The blouse waist is in four pieces: Front, Back, Sleeve and Cuff. Gather the front to fit the neck, face the bottom, and insert a rubber cord.

The under waist is in two pieces: Front and Back. Close in the back with buttons and button-holes.

The skirt is drafted by the scale corresponding with the waist measure. Lay the pleats according to the notches. Press carefully and sew to the under-waist.

Regulate the length by the tape measure.

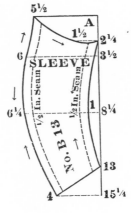

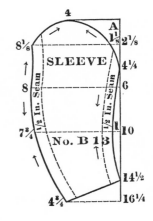

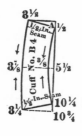

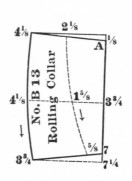

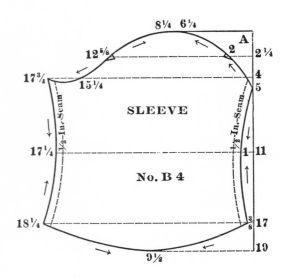

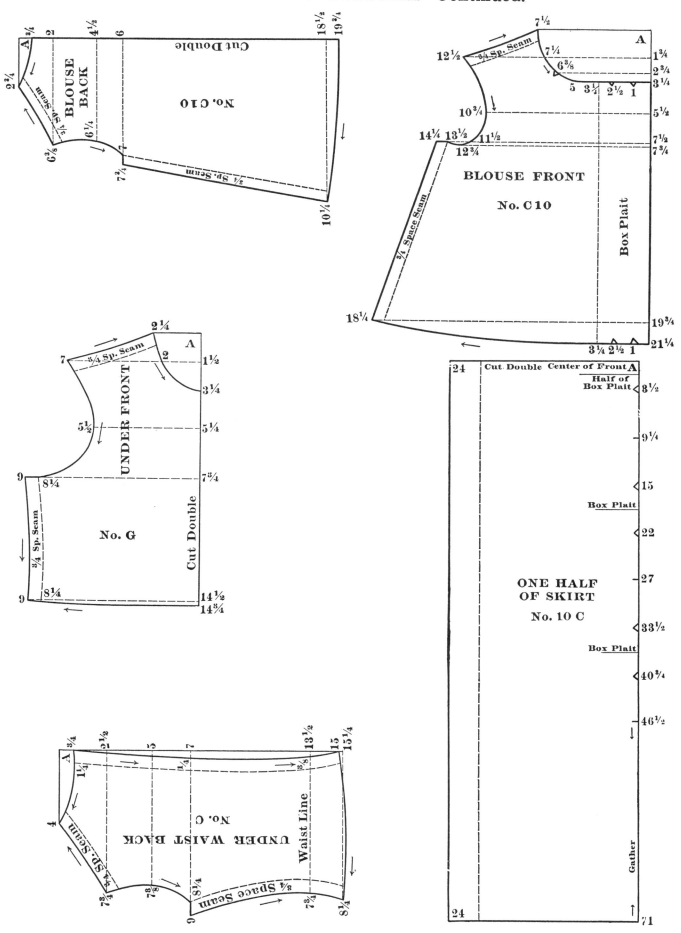

LADIES' STREET COSTUME.

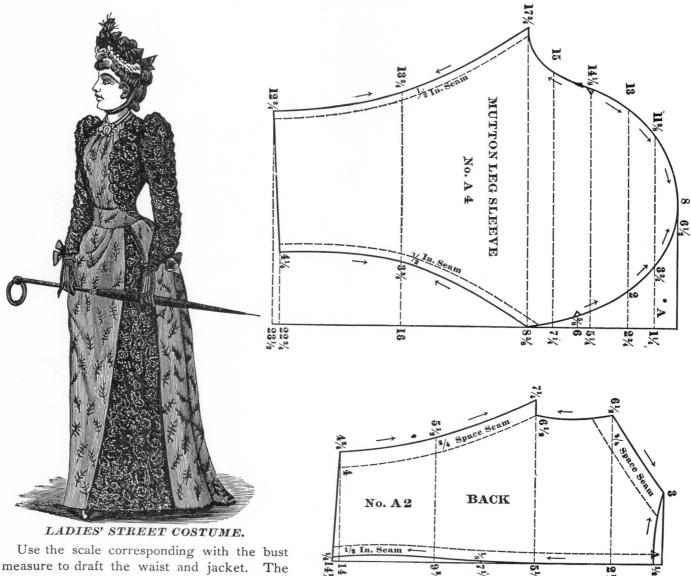

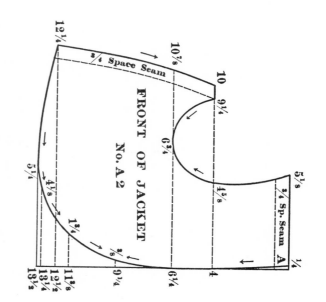

LADIES' STREET COSTUME.

Use the scale corresponding with the bust measure to draft the waist and jacket. The waist consists of Upper and Under Front, Back, Side Back, and Under-arm-gore.

The full front is simply turned down at the top and shirred one or more times. Gather the bottom between the notches and join to the under front at the under arm and shoulder seams. Finish the bottom of the waist with a pointed or rounding belt. The sleeves may be made of the same material as the waist, if preferred. The Jacket consists of two pieces: Front and Back. Make it as long in the back as the waist can be made, of velvet or lace.

The drapery is given on page 14. Draft out by the scale corresponding with the waist measure. Is in two pieces: Front and Back. Lay the pleats according to the notches; make it as long as the skirt.

Draft the skirt from any of the plain skirt patterns given in this issue.

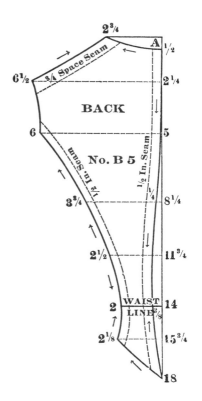

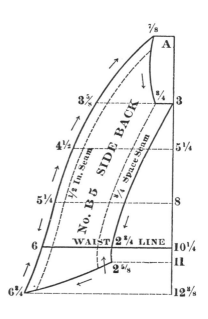

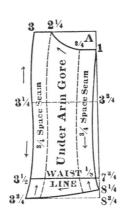

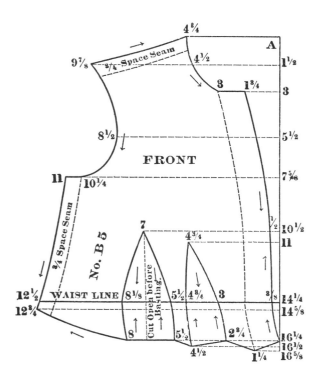

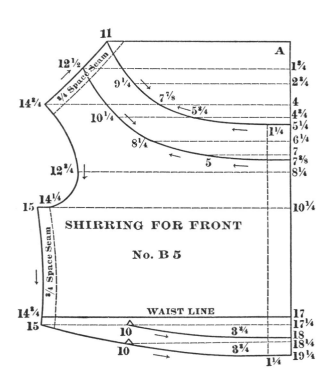

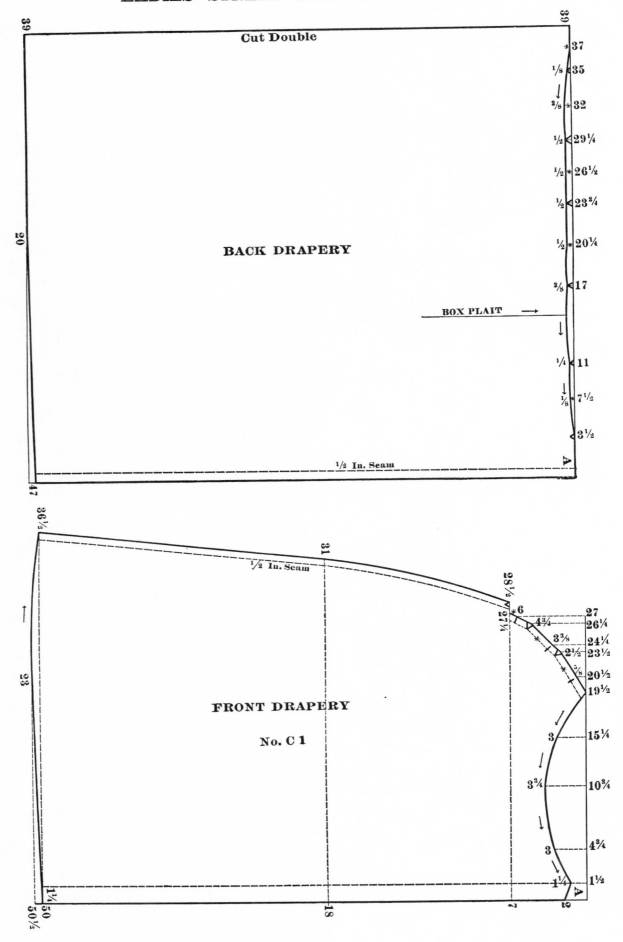

BACK DRAPERY

Cut Double

BOX PLAIT →

FRONT DRAPERY

No. C 1

LADIES' STREET COSTUME.

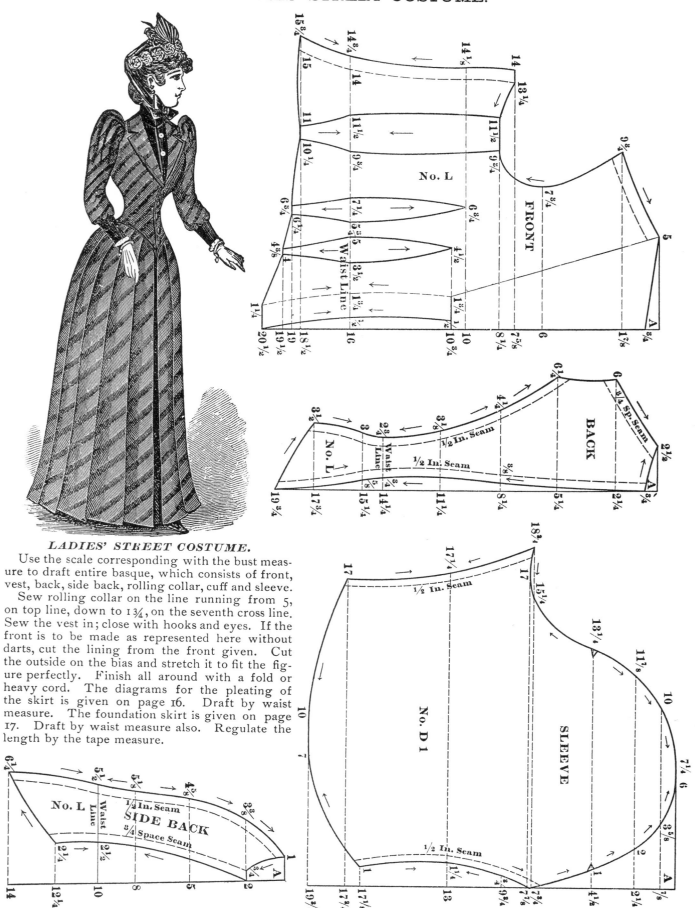

LADIES' STREET COSTUME.

Use the scale corresponding with the bust measure to draft entire basque, which consists of front, vest, back, side back, rolling collar, cuff and sleeve.

Sew rolling collar on the line running from 5, on top line, down to 1¾, on the seventh cross line. Sew the vest in; close with hooks and eyes. If the front is to be made as represented here without darts, cut the lining from the front given. Cut the outside on the bias and stretch it to fit the figure perfectly. Finish all around with a fold or heavy cord. The diagrams for the pleating of the skirt is given on page 16. Draft by waist measure. The foundation skirt is given on page 17. Draft by waist measure also. Regulate the length by the tape measure.

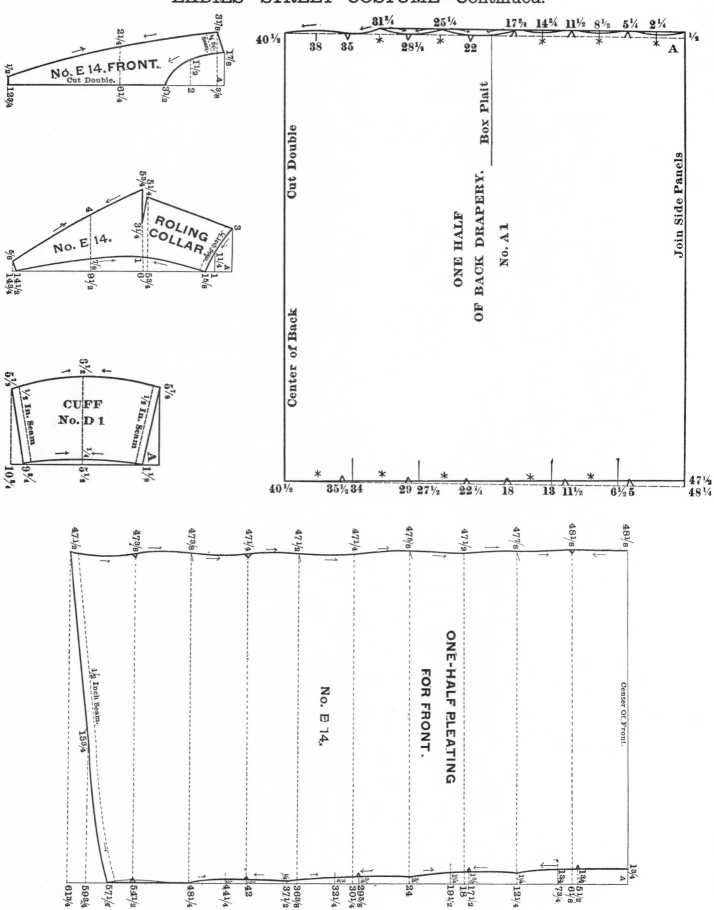

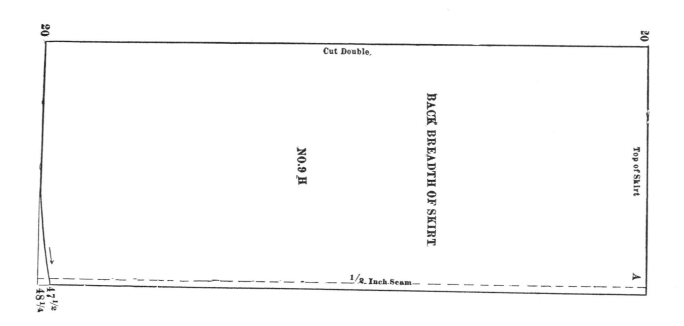

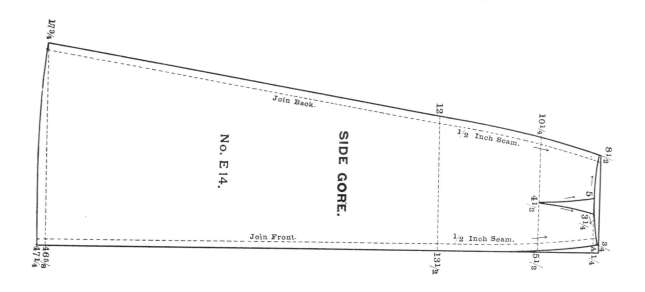

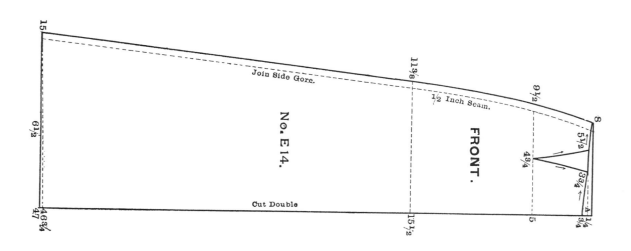

MISSES' CLOAK.

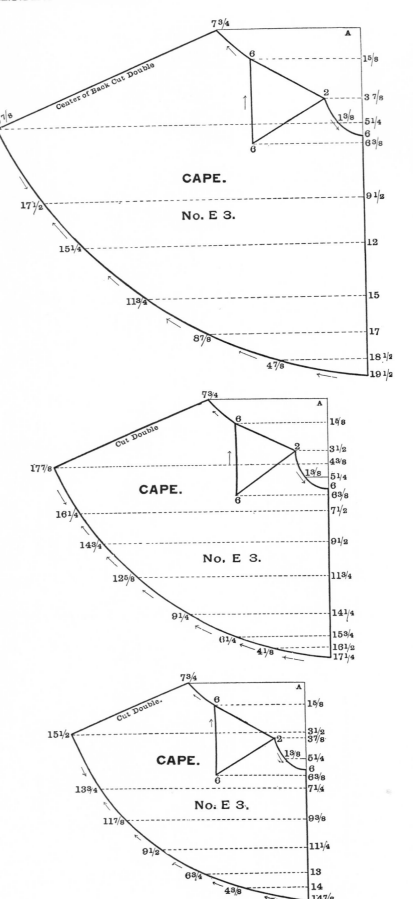

CAPE.

No. E 3.

Center of Back Cut Double

7¾
A
6
1⅝
2
3⅞
1⅜
5¼
6
6⅜
19⅞
6
9½
17½
12
15¼
15
11¾
17
8⅞
18½
4⅞
19½

CAPE.

No. E 3.

Cut Double

7¾
A
6
1⅝
2
3½
4⅜
1⅜
5¼
6
6⅜
17⅞
6
7½
16¼
9½
14¾
11¾
12⅝
14¼
9¼
15¾
6¼
16½
4⅛
17¼

CAPE.

No. E 3.

Cut Double.

7¾
A
6
1⅝
2
3½
3⅞
1⅜
5¼
6
6⅜
15½
7¼
6
13¾
9⅜
11⅞
11¼
9½
13
6¾
14
4⅜
14⅞

MISSES' CLOAK.

Use the scale corresponding with the bust measure to draft the entire garment, which consists of front, back, side-back, two sleeves, cuff and three cape portions.

Draft the same as all other garments, put the parts together as they are marked, take up the dart on the shoulders of the cape.

Make of any suitable material.

Regulate the length by the tape measure.

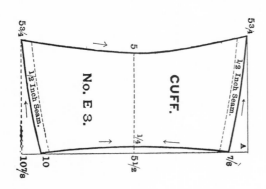

5¾
5¾
5
No. E 3.
CUFF.
½ Inch Seam.
½ Inch Seam.
¼
¼
10⅞
10
5½
⅞
A

MISSES' CLOAK—Continued.

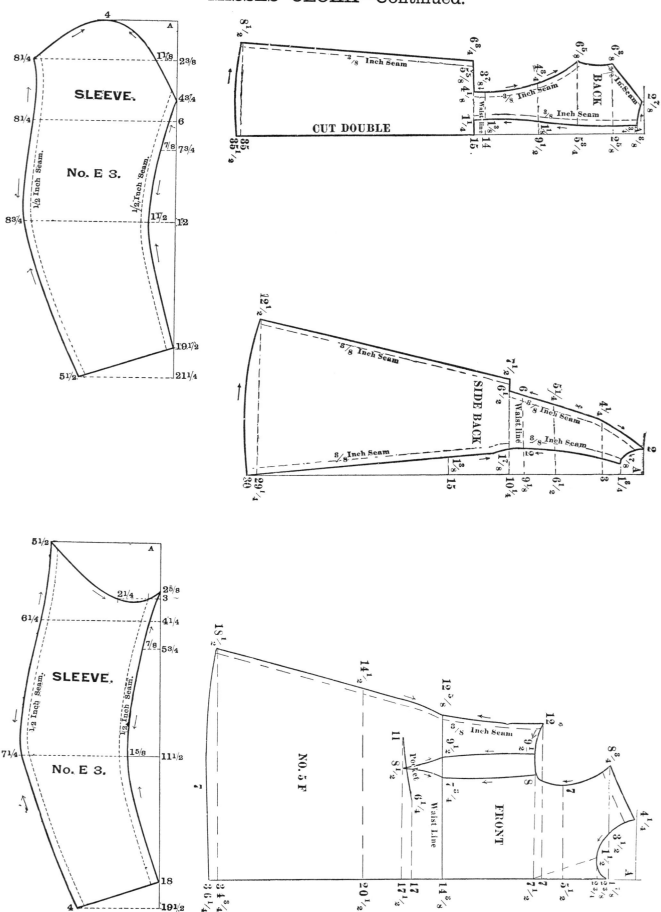

LADIES' TRAIN WRAPPER.

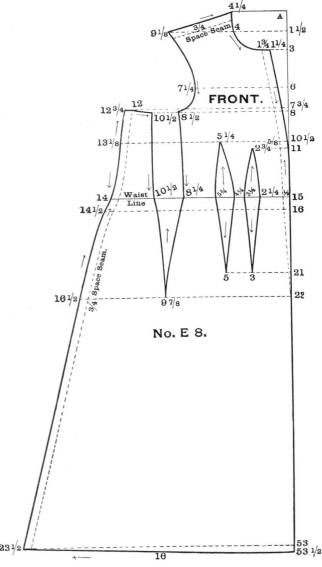

FRONT.

No. E 8.

LADIES' TRAIN WRAPPER.

Use the scale corresponding with the the bust measure to draft the entire garment, which consists of front, back, side back, collar and two sleeve portions.

Lay the pleats in the back according to the notches.

Close in front with hooks and eyes; trim the foot with a pleated ruche, made of the same material as the dress. This may extend just across the front or all around.

Regulate the length to suit.

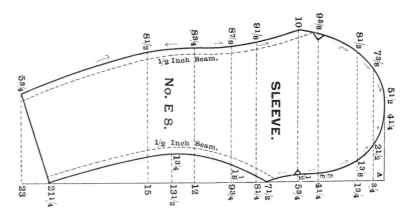

SLEEVE.

No. E 8.

LADIES' TRAIN WRAPPER—Continued.

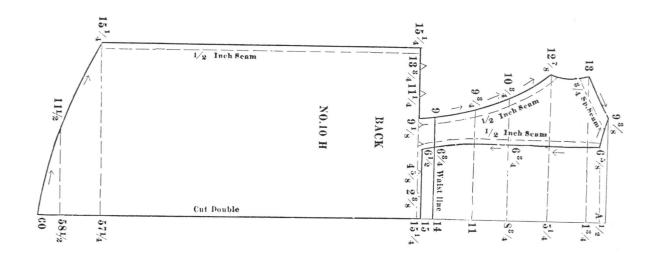

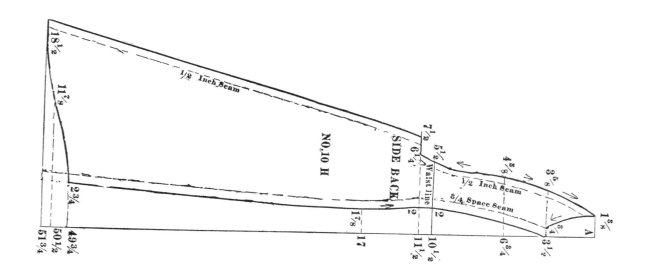

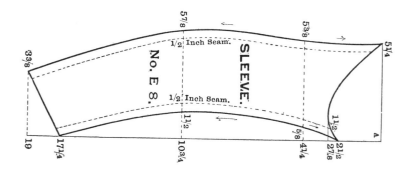

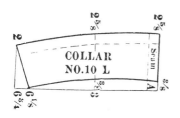

CHILD'S COSTUME.

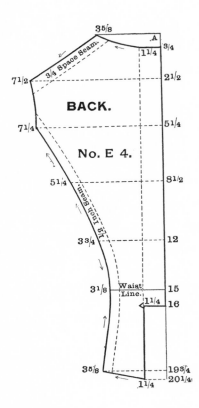

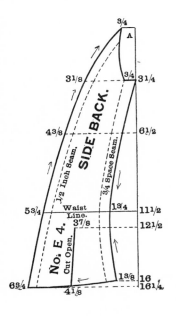

CHILD'S COSTUME.

Use the scale corresponding with the bust measure to draft the waist and sleeves, which consists of front, back side-back, under-arm-gore, collar, cuff and three sleeve portions. Cut the bottom as represented. Trim same as the skirt, close in the back, with buttons and button-holes; cut the lining for the sleeves from the smaller patterns. The skirt is drafted by the scale corresponding with the waist measure; lay the pleats according to the notches. Regulate the length by the tape measure.

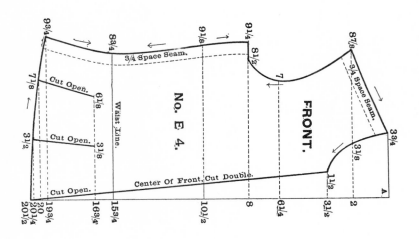

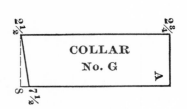

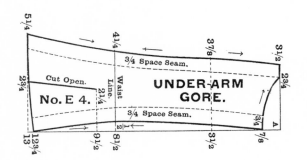

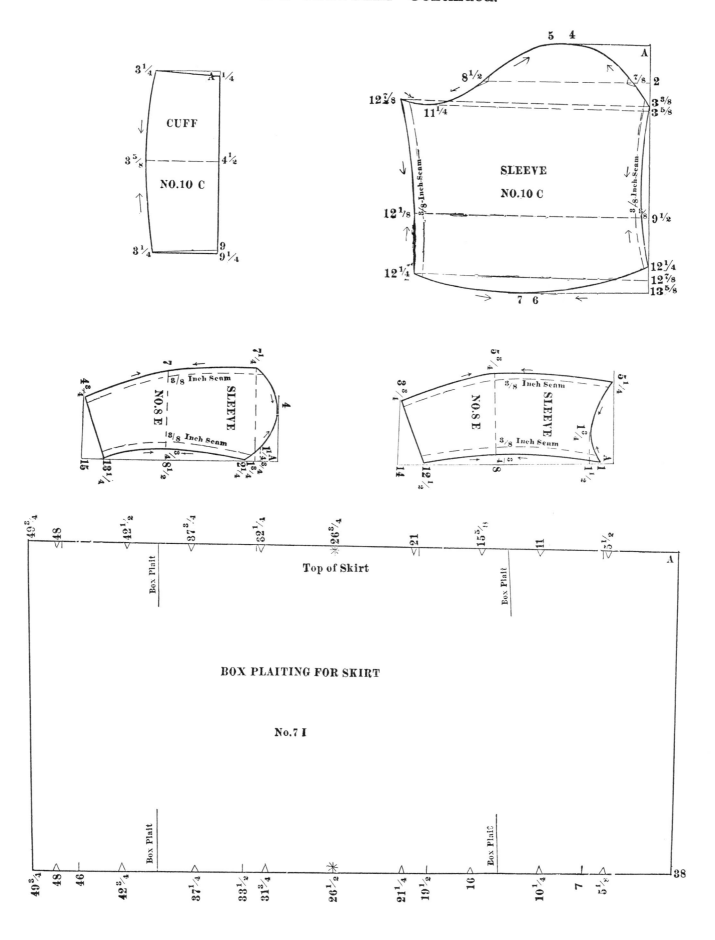

LADIES' WRAP.

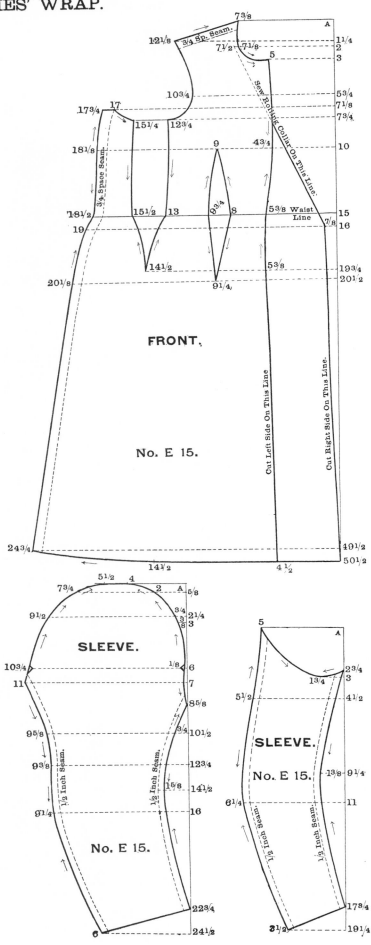

FRONT.

No. E 15.

SLEEVE.

No. E 15.

SLEEVE.

No. E 15.

LADIES' LONG WRAP.

Use the scale corresponding with the bust measure to draft the entire garment, which consists of front, back, side back, collar and two sleeve portions. Cut on the inside line for the left front and the outside line for the right front. Trim with fur or astrachan.

The polonaise, given on page 26, is drafted by bust measure. It consists of right and left front, back, side back, under-arm-gore, cuff and sleeve, which are given on page 25. Lay the pleats in the front according to the notches; lay two double box pleats in the back; trim as desired. The skirt is drafted by the waist measure and is in three pieces: Front, back, side gore. Regulate to suit.

LADIES' WRAP—Continued.

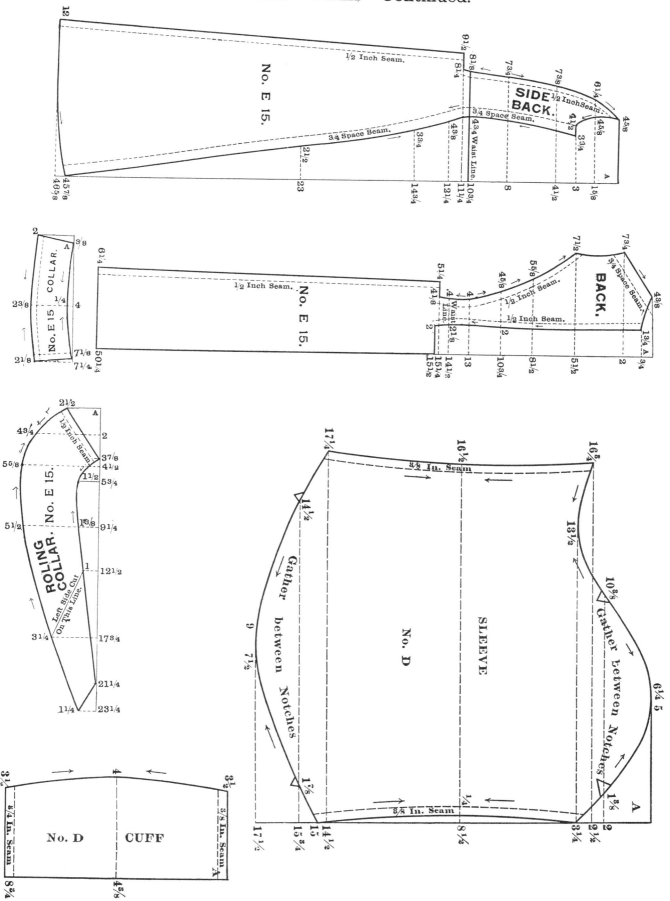

LADIES' POLONAISE.

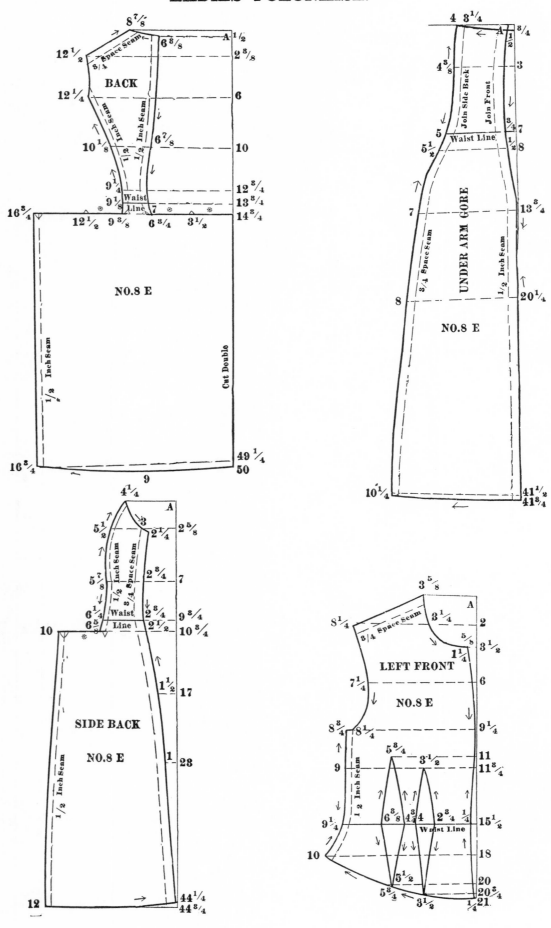

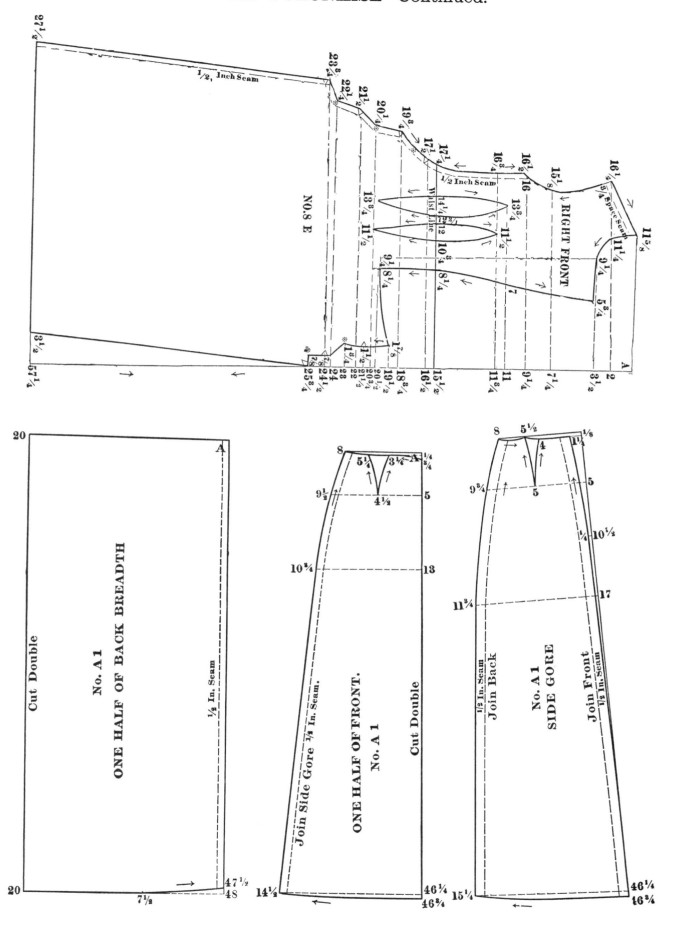

MISSES' COSTUME.

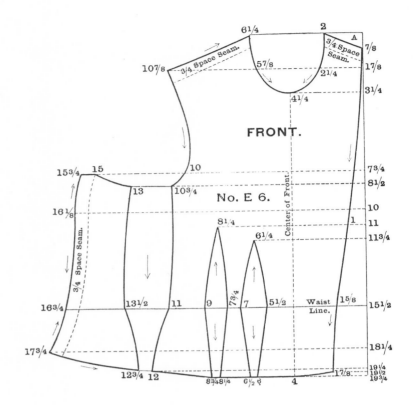

MISSES' COSTUME.

Use the scale corresponding with the bust measure to draft the basque and sleeves, which consist of front, back and side back and sleeve.

This is a straight, round basque with diagonal front.

The skirt is given on page 29. Draft by the waist measure; is in one piece; gather very full in the back. Any style of trimming may be used. Regulate the length by the tape measure.

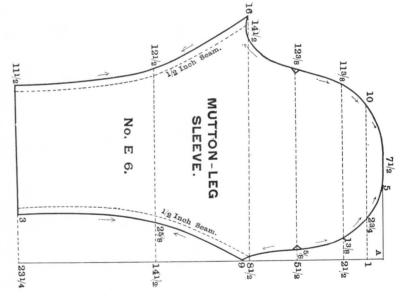

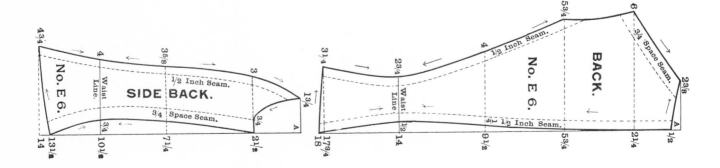

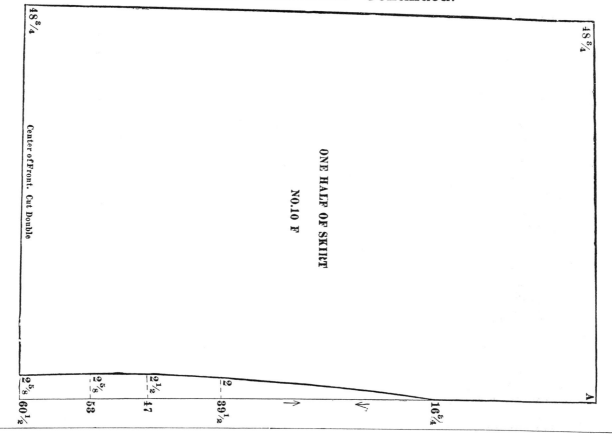

ONE HALF OF SKIRT

NO.10 F

Center of Front. Cut Double

48 3/4

48 3/4

A

16 3/4

2 — 39 1/2

2 1/2 — 47

2 5/8 — 53

2 5/8 — 60 1/2

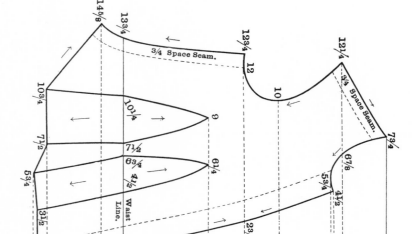

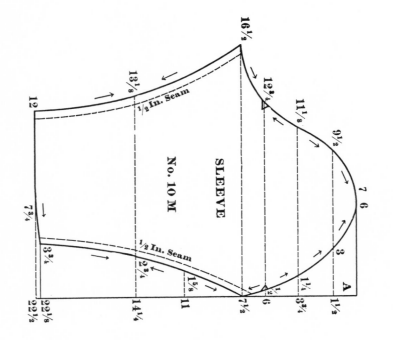

LADIES' STREET COSTUME.

Use the bust measure to draft the basque, which consists of five pieces: Front, back, side-back, under-arm-gore, and sleeve.

This basque gives the bias effect. In cutting the front lay the front edge of the pattern on the straight edge of the goods, which will bring it bias under the arm.

The skirt is given on page 31. Draft by the waist measure; is in two pieces, front and back. Lay the pleats in the front according to the notches, lay the back in two double box pleats, cut the foundation skirt from any plain skirt pattern, trim the bottom of the skirt with pleating, velvet, astrachan or braiding. Regulate the length by the tape measure.

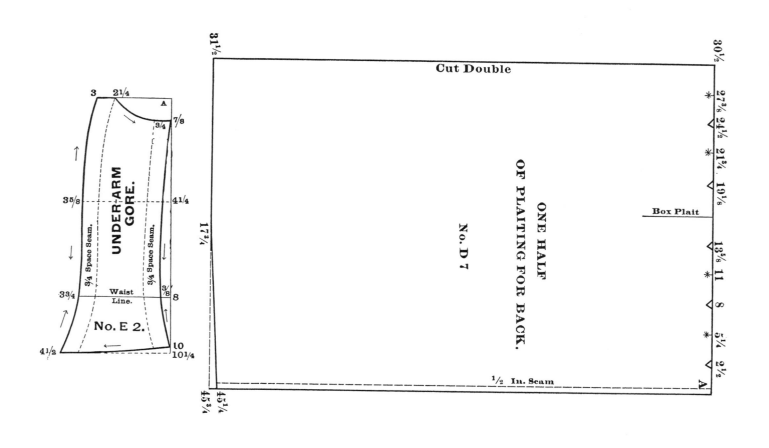

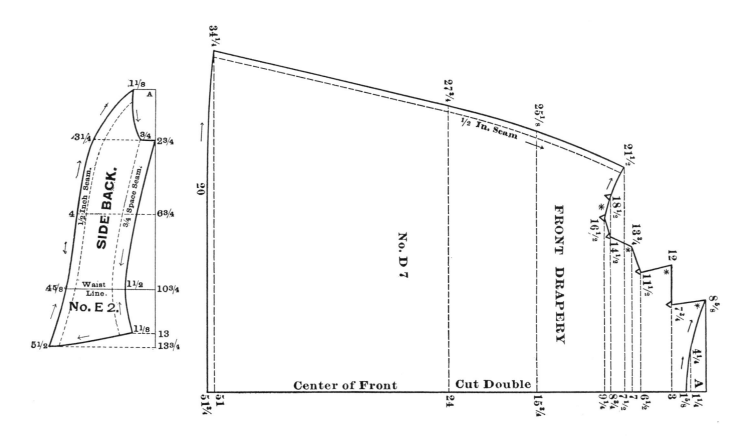

LADIES' COSTUME.

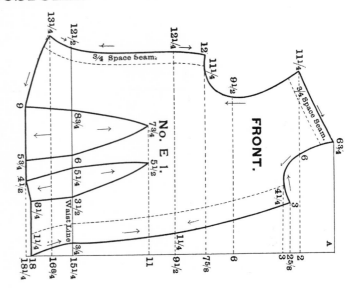

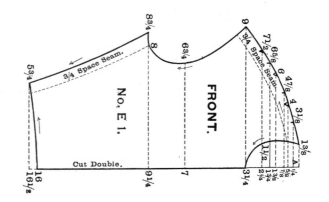

LADIES' COSTUME.

Use the scale corresponding with the bust measure to draft the entire waist, which consists of upper and under front, upper and under back, side back, under-arm-gore and two sleeve portions. Cut the entire costume on the bias. Lay the pleats on the shoulder according to the notches. Close the under front or lining down the center of the front. Face the upper front on the left side from the neck to the waist, and close with buttons on the left shoulder and uuder the arms. Finish bottom with a velvet girdle or velvet ribbon, with a bow and long ends in the back. The skirt is in one piece. Draft with waist measure. Lay the pleats in front according to the notches; gather the back very full and sew to the waist.

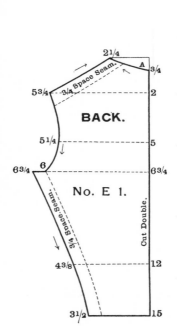

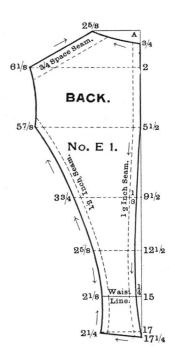

LADIES' COSTUME—Continued.

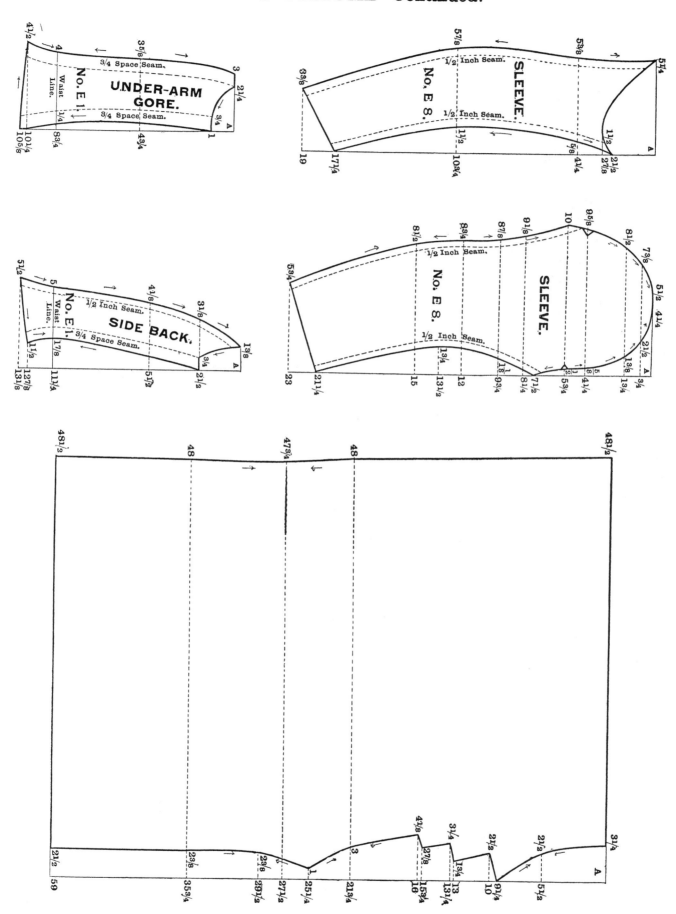

BOY'S SUIT.

BOYS' COSTUME.

Use the scale corresponding with the bust measure to draft the entire coat and under waist. The coat consists of front, back, collar and two sleeves. The under waist is in two pieces, front and back. Draft this the same as all other garments. Finish the edges of the coat with a binding or stitching. Draft the skirt by the waist measure. Lay the pleats according to the notches, one large box pleat in the front and smaller ones in the back. Press carefully and sew to the waist. Regulate the length by the tape measure.

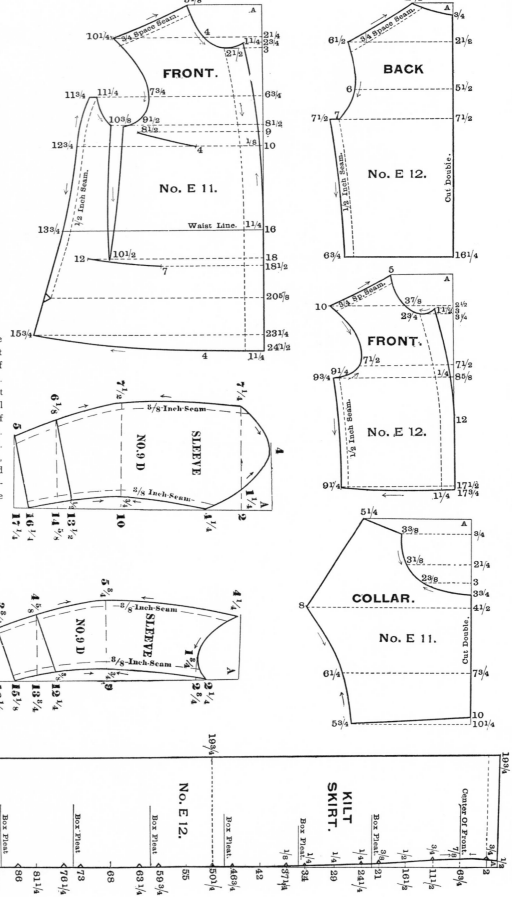

LADIES' STREET COSTUME.

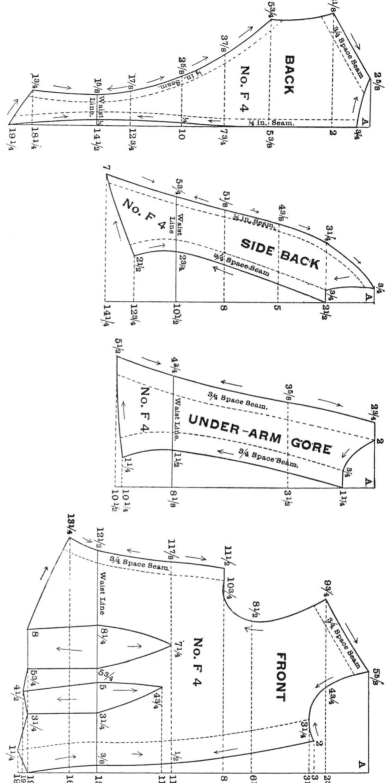

Use the scale corresponding with the Bust measure to draft the entire Basque, which consists of Front, Back, Side-back, Under-arm Gore, Collar and Sleeve portions. Any style of trimming may be used on the waist that is desirable. If made of large plaid, no trimming is required. Gather the sleeves very full just on top. Put a layer of wadding on the upper part to make it stand up nicely. Cut the sleeves on the bias.

The drapery is given on page 37. Draft by the waist measure. Is in two pieces, front and back. Make the pleats on the front to come on the right or left side, just to suit the wearer. The back is laid in two double box pleats.

The diagrams for the underskirt are given on page 36. Draft by the waist measure. Trim to suit. Regulate length by the tape measure.

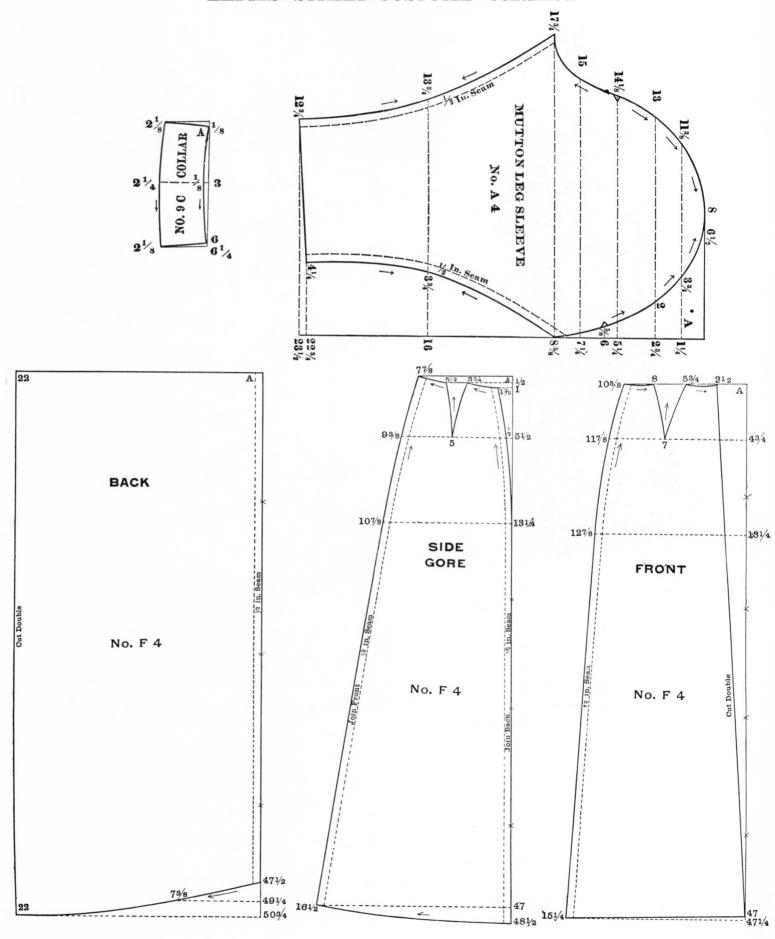

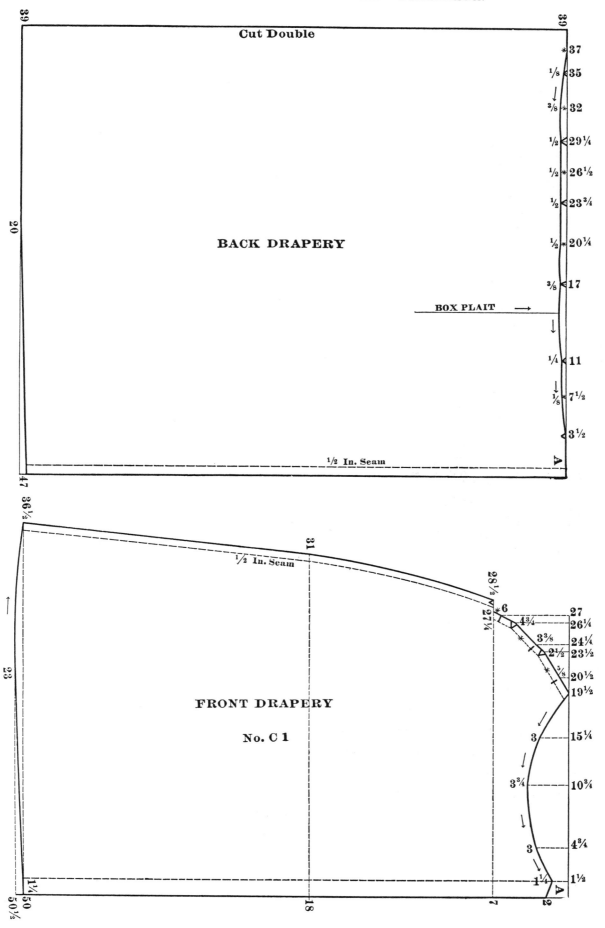

Cut Double

39   39

* 37

¹⁄₈   35

³⁄₈   * 32

¹⁄₂   29¼

¹⁄₂   * 26½

¹⁄₂   23¾

¹⁄₂   * 20¼

BACK DRAPERY

20

³⁄₈   17

BOX PLAIT →

¹⁄₄   11

¹⁄₈   * 7½

3½

½ In. Seam   A

47

36½

31   ½ In. Seam

28½   27¼

* 6   27

4¾   26¼

*   3⅜   24¼

2½   23½

*   ⅝   20½

19½

FRONT DRAPERY

No. C 1

23

3   15¼

3¾   10¾

3   4¾

1¼   1½

A

1¼   50

50½

18   7   2

LADIES' HOUSE DRESS.

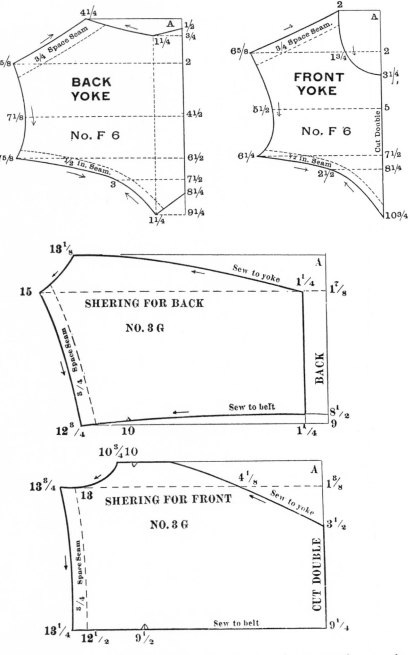

Draft the waist and sleeves by the scale corresponding with the bust measure, it consists of yoke and shirring for front and back' collar and two sleeve portions

Gather the shirring portions at the top and sew to the yoke. Gather the bottom between the notches and sew to the belt. This may be made to open in the back for a miss or in front for a lady. If it is made to open in front take the hem off the back and cut the goods double, and allow the hem in front 1 ¼ space hem. Gather the sleeves at the top between the notches.

Draft the skirt by the scale corresponding with the waist measure, it consists of front and back. Take up the darts in front, lay small pleats in the back turning toward the center of the back. Do not make the back over 6 inches wide after it is all pleated. Trim the bottom to suit. Regulate the length by the tape measure.

LADIES' HOUSE DRESS—Continued.

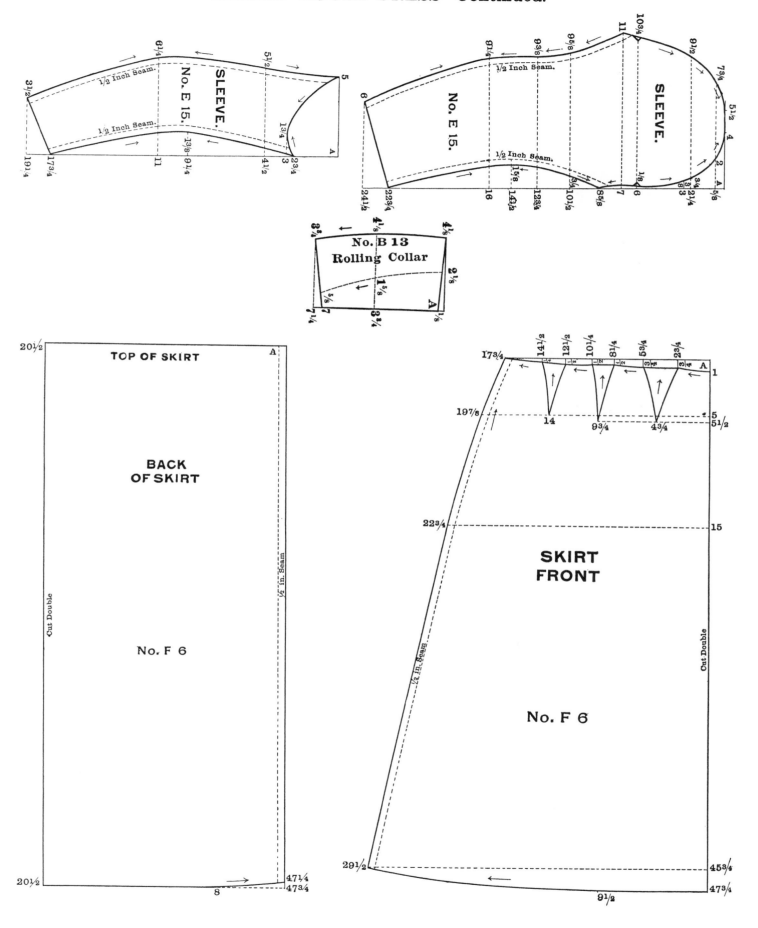

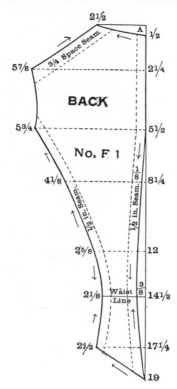

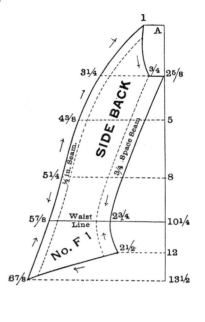

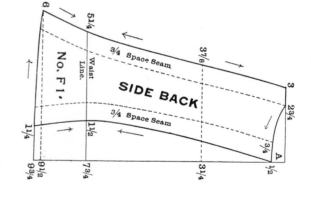

Use the scale corresponding with the Bust measure to draft the entire Basque, which consists of two Fronts, two Backs, Side-back, Under-arm-gore, two gathered portions Collar, Cuff and Sleeve.

The Basque can be made of plain white goods. The center front and back, and the gathered portions are made of the embroidery. Bring the fullness nearly all on the shoulder. Gather the sleeves be- ween the notches.

The skirt is given on page 42. Draft by the waist measure. Trim the front with embroidery flouncing, or simply make it of the embroidery skirting. Bring the full- ness in the back. Or it may be made of plain goods with one, two or three ruffles of the embroidery. Regulate the length to suit.

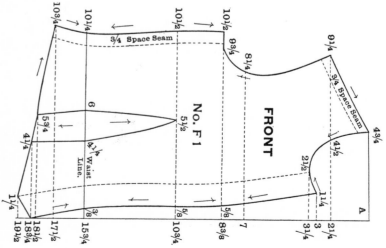

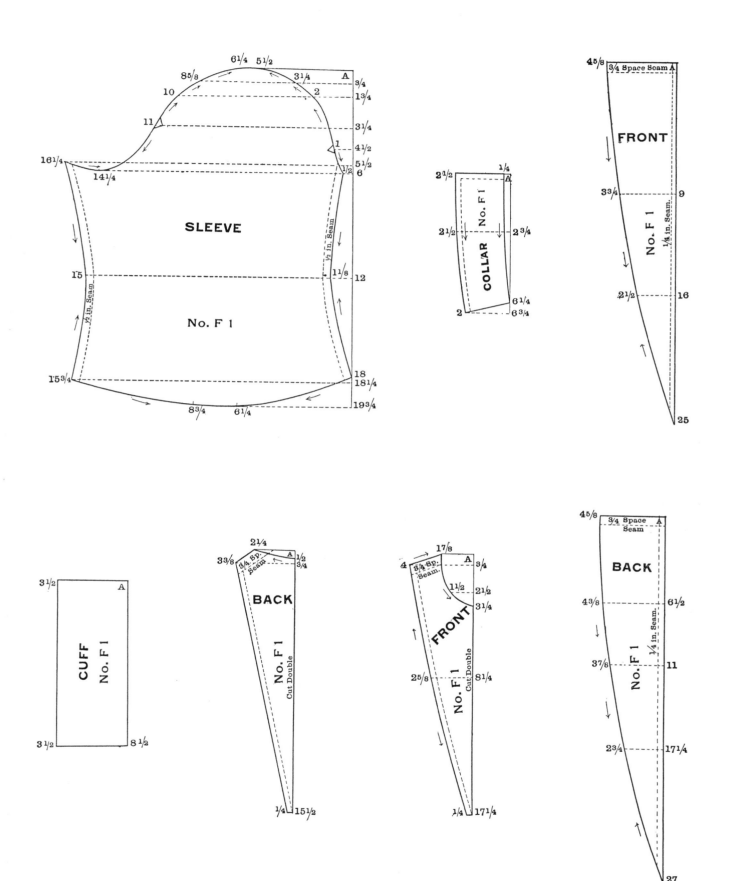

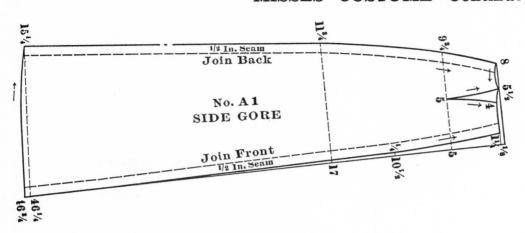

No. A 1
SIDE GORE

½ In. Seam
Join Back

Join Front
½ In. Seam

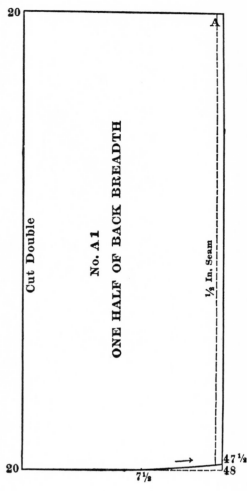

No. A 1
ONE HALF OF BACK BREADTH

Cut Double

½ In. Seam

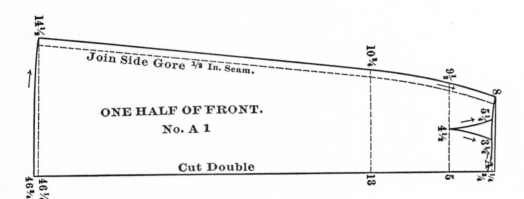

Join Side Gore ½ In. Seam.

ONE HALF OF FRONT.
No. A 1

Cut Double

CHILD'S CHEMISE AND DRAWERS.

Use the scale corresponding with the bust measure to draft the chemise, which consists of one piece. The back and front are cut alike. Regulate the length to suit.

The drawers are drafted by the waist measure. Make allowance for the tucks.

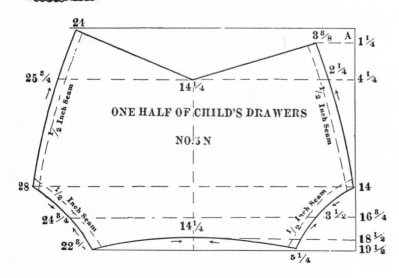

ONE HALF OF CHILD'S DRAWERS

NO. 5 N

½ Inch Seam

½ Inch Seam

½ Inch Seam

½ Inch Seam

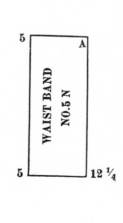

WAIST BAND
NO. 5 N

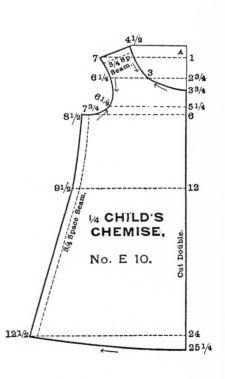

¼ CHILD'S
CHEMISE.

No. E 10.

Cut Double

¾ Space Seam.

¾ Sp. Seam.

CHILD'S STREET COSTUME.

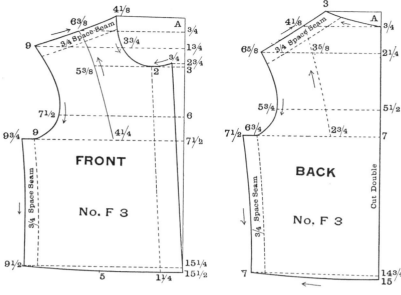

FRONT

No. F 3

BACK

No. F 3

Cut Double

Use the scale corresponding with the Bust measure to draft the entire waist, which consists of upper and under fronts and backs.

Turn the upper portions down on the first dotted line. Shirr on the second line and sew to the dotted line on the under front and back. Get sleeve diagrams on page 44 of this issue, or any other sleeve desirable.

The skirt is drafted by the waist measure; is in one piece; only one-half of the skirt is given. There are two large box pleats, one on each side. Side pleating in the front and back. This is a beautiful little costume when properly made.

Regulate the length to suit.

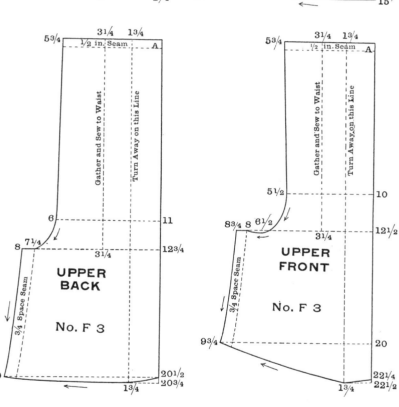

UPPER BACK

No. F 3

Gather and Sew to Waist

Turn Away on this Line

UPPER FRONT

No. F 3

Gather and Sew to Waist

Turn Away on this Line

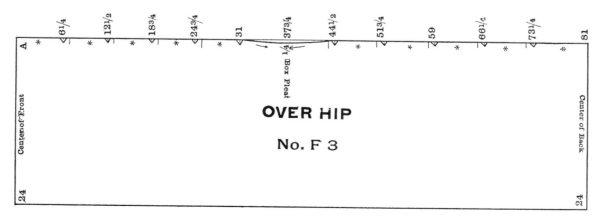

OVER HIP

No. F 3

Center of Front

Center of Back

Box Pleat

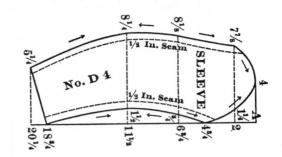

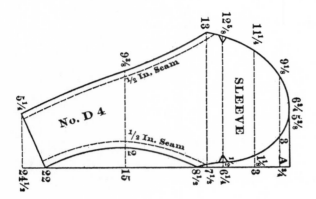

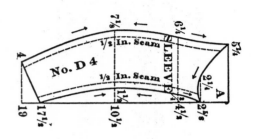

GENTLEMEN'S NIGHT SHIRT.

Use the scale corresponding with the chest measure.

Is in five pieces: Front, Back, Collar, Pocket and one-half of Sleeve.

We deem it unnecessary to give a description of the different parts, as any seamstress will know how to put the different parts together. The seams are all marked.

The front is cut open down to the notch at 15 on base line.

The sleeve and cuff are cut together. Gather the sleeve at the top to fit the arm size.

Regulate the length with the tape line.

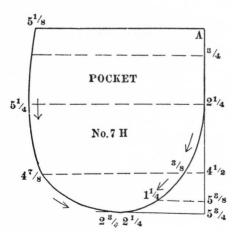

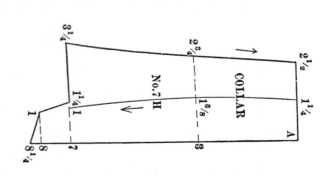

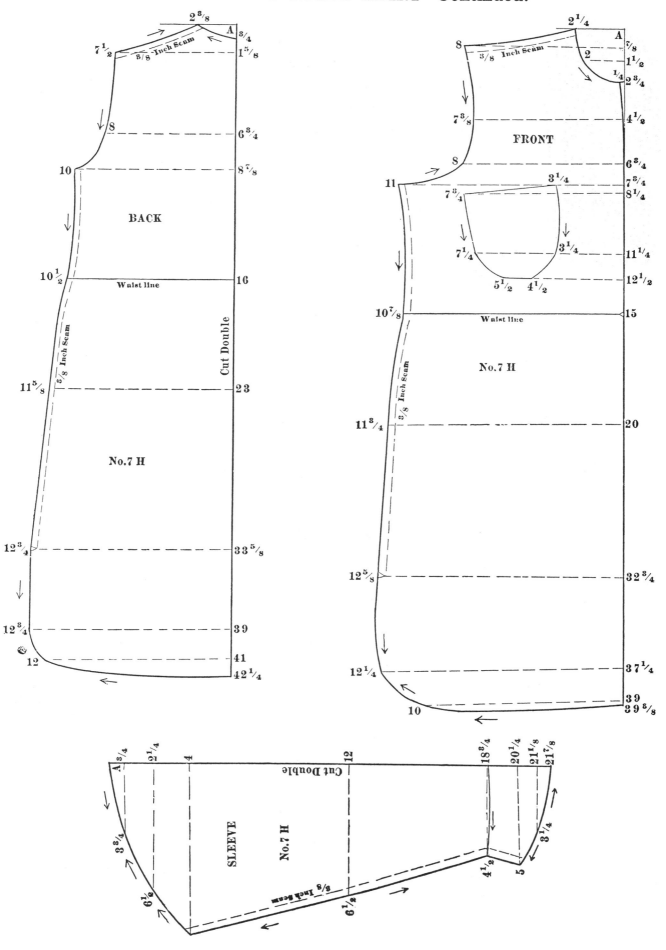

GENTLEMEN'S DRESSING GOWN.

Use scale corresponding with the chest measure.

Is in eight pieces: Front, Back, Collar, two Pocket Laps and two Sleeve portions.

Is drafted upon the general plan.

Regulate the length by the use of the tape measure.

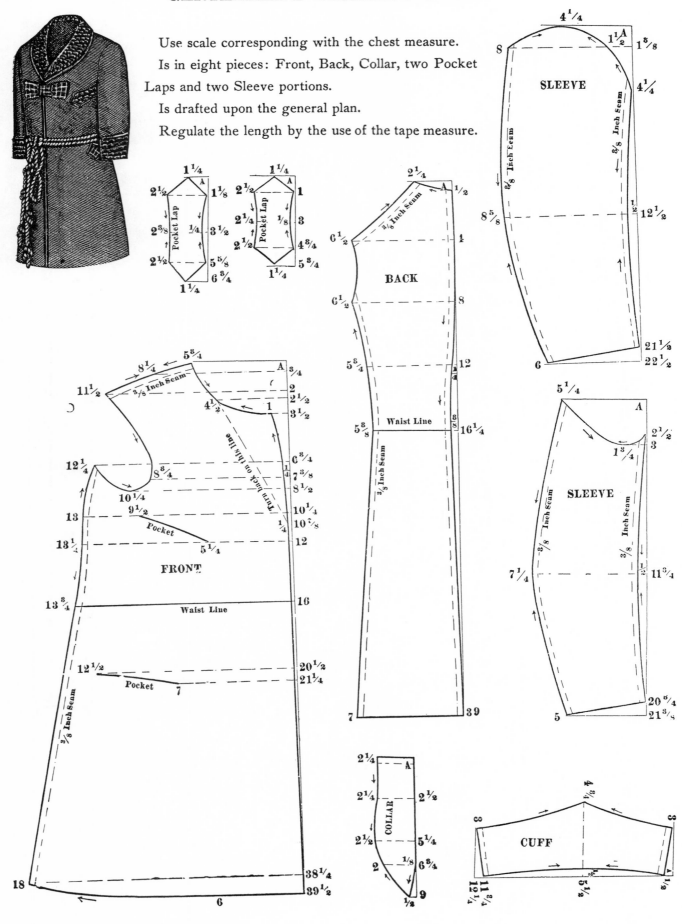

LADIES' SACK NIGHT GOWN.

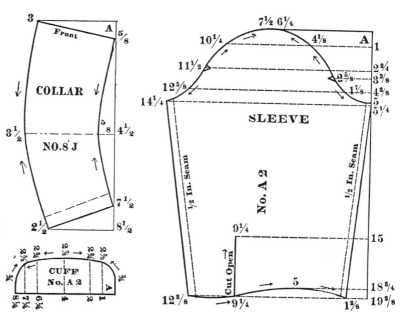

Use the scale corresponding with the bust measure to draft the entire garment, which consists of five pieces: Front, Back, Collar Sleeve and Cuff.

This is drafted out the same as all other garments. Gather the sleeve at the bottom and sew to the cuff, and gather between the notches at the top and sew in the arm's eye. Regulate the length by the tape measure.

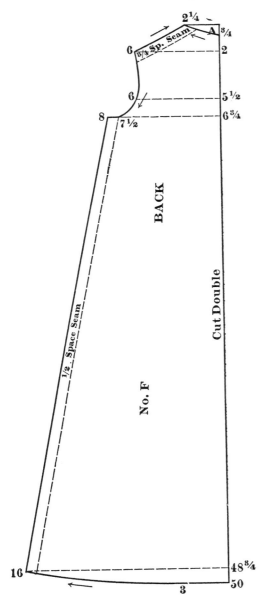

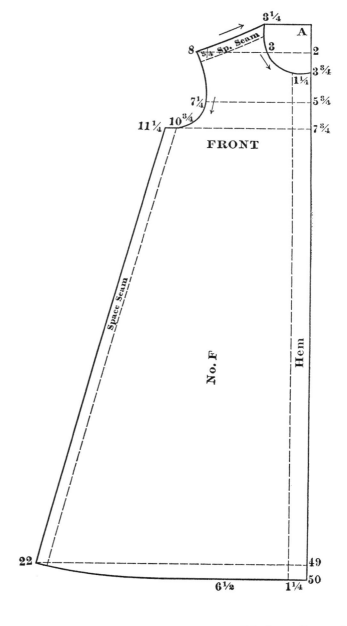

LADIES' HOUSE DRESS.

Center of Back   Cut Double

ONE HALF
OF BACK DRAPERY.

No. A1

Box Plait

Join Side Panels

Use the scale corresponding with the bust measure to draft the waist and sleeves, which consists of front and back yoke, shirring for front and back, collar, cuff and sleeve. Gather the shirred portions at the top and sew to the yoke. Lay in side pleats at the waist line. Hem or face the bottom. Gather or pleat the sleeves between the notches. Gather the bottom and sew to the cuff.

Draft the skirt with the scale corresponding with the waist measure. Lay the pleats according to the notches, turn the pleats toward the center of the front, make two double box pleats in the back. Regulate the length to suit.

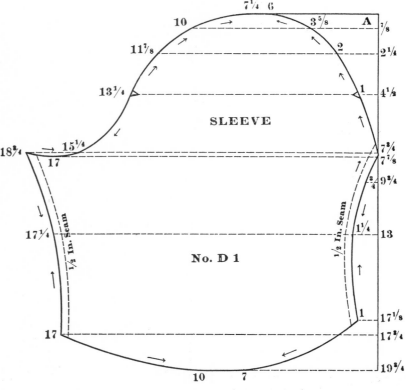

SLEEVE

No. D 1

1/2 In. Seam

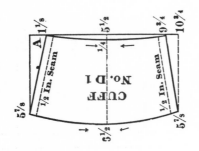

CUFF
No. D 1

1/2 In. Seam

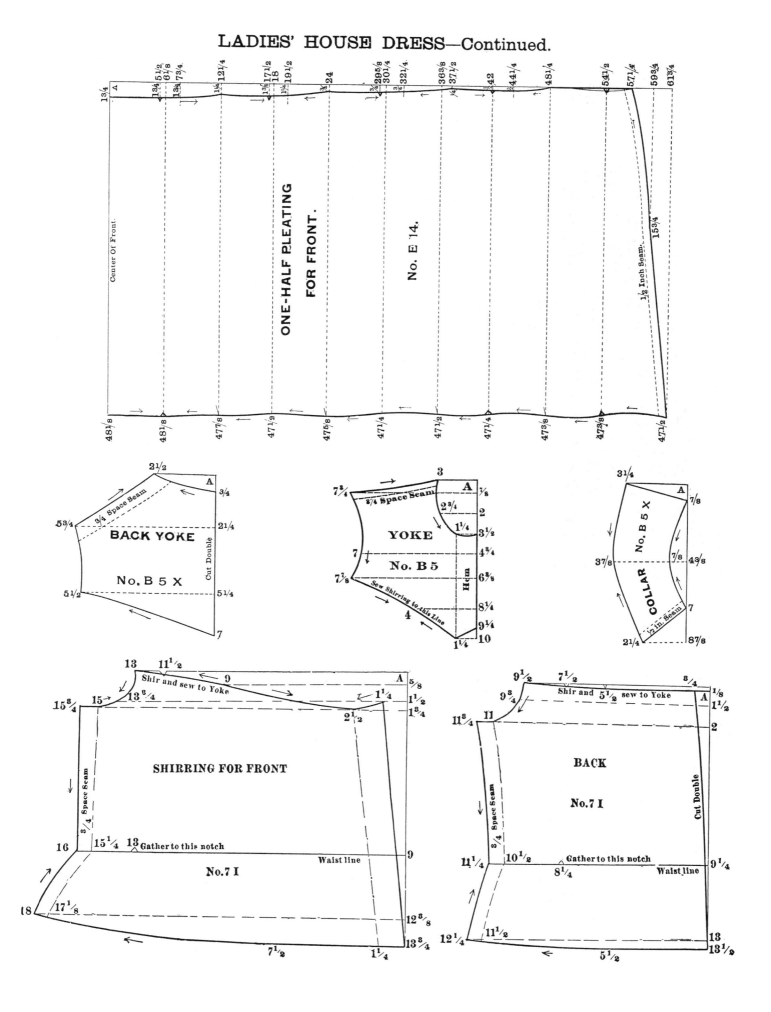

LADIES' STREET COSTUME.

Use the scale corresponding with the bust measure to draft the entire waist and jacket. The jacket consists of front, back, side-back, under-arm-gore, collar, facing for front and two sleeve portions. Cut the desired length. The diagrams for the sleeves are given on page 52 of this issue. Gather or pleat very full on the top between the notches. The waist is given on page 51. There are two fronts, back, side-back, under-arm-gore and collar. Use any sleeve desirable. Shirr the upper front at the neck and waist. The diagrams for the drapery are shown on page 52. Draft the waist measure. Lay the pleats according to the notches. Make the length of the skirt. Use the scale corresponding with the waist measure to draft the skirt, is given on page 53 of this issue. This skirt is made with a yoke. Regulate the length with the tape measure.

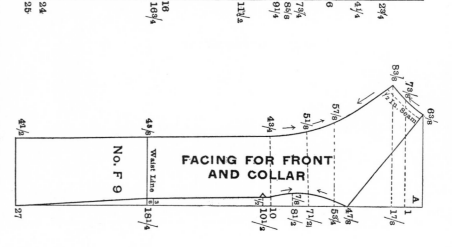

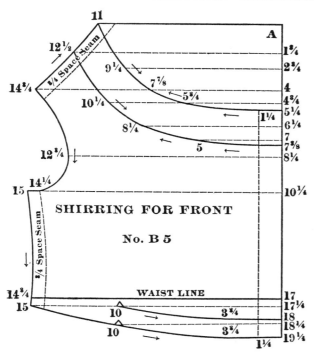

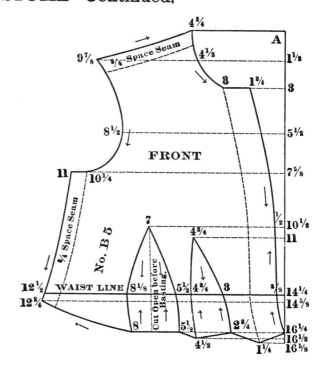

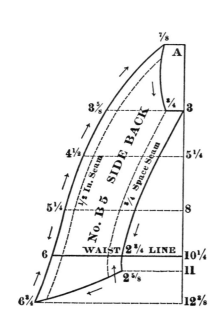

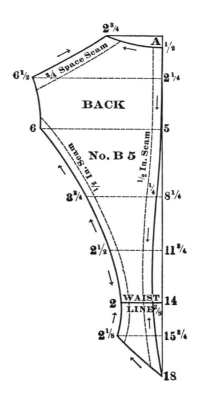

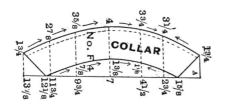

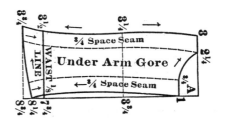

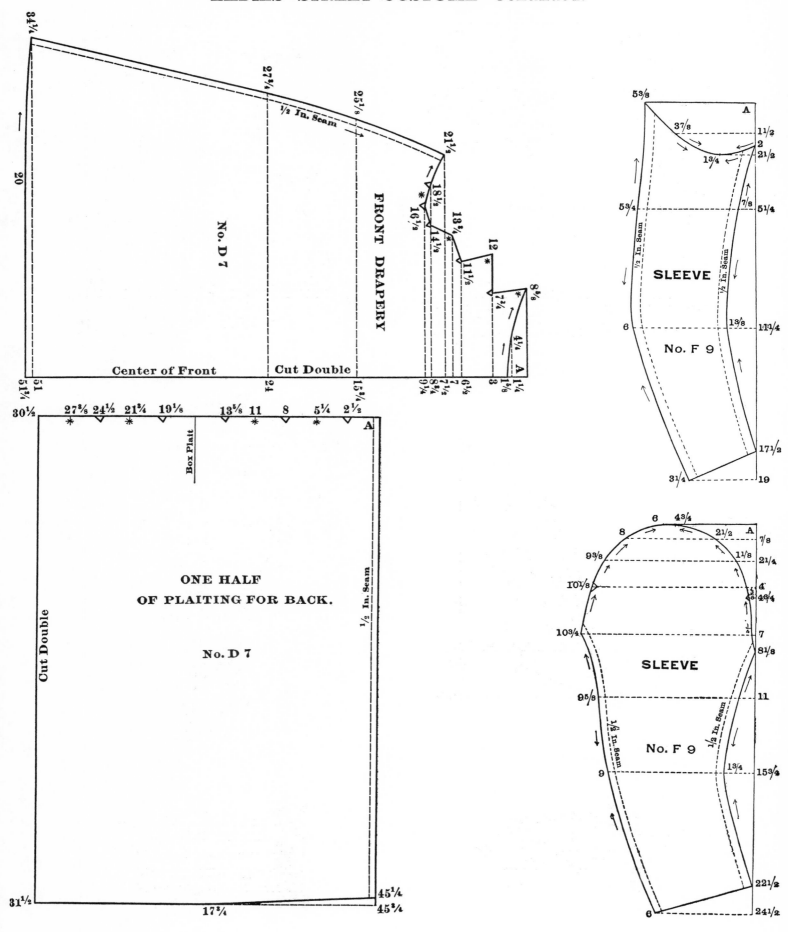

No. D 7

FRONT DRAPERY

Center of Front   Cut Double

ONE HALF
OF PLAITING FOR BACK.

No. D 7

Cut Double

Box Plait

SLEEVE

No. F 9

SLEEVE

No. F 9

LADIES' YOKE SKIRT.

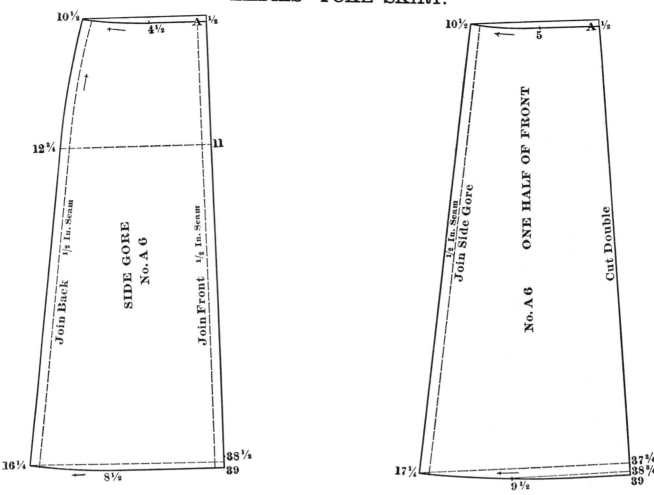

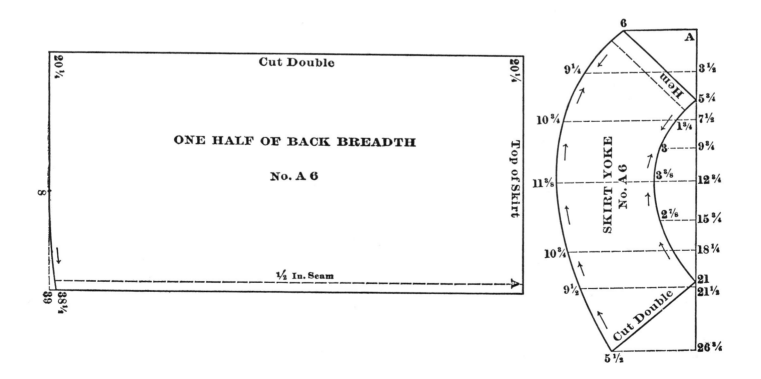

LADIES' STREET COSTUME.

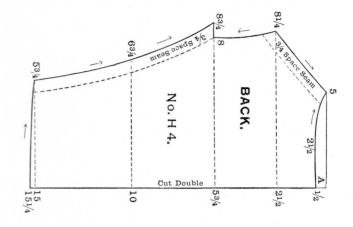

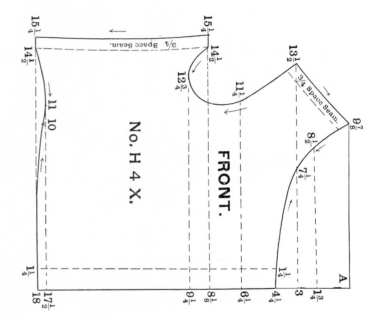

Draft the entire waist by the scale corresponding with the Bust measure. It consists of Front and Back and two portions for the yoke lining, collar and three sleeve portions. Shirr the front and back at the neck as many times as desired and sew to the lining.

The sleeves are given on page 55. Gather or pleat the large portion, or Balloon sleeve, from one point to the other, not the old-fashioned way of gathering, just on the top to make it stand up high; the new sleeves are not high, but flat and full to give them a broad appearance.

The skirt is given on page 56. Draft by the waist measure. Any other skirt may be used if more desirable. The skirts are very wide this spring. The one piece skirt is used very much, making it five yards wide at the bottom. Gather the back very full. Regulate length by the tape-measure.

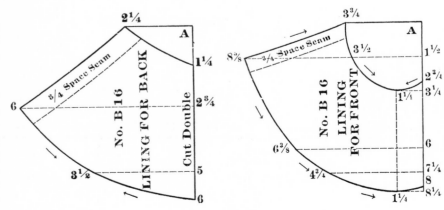

LADIES' STREET COSTUME—Continued.

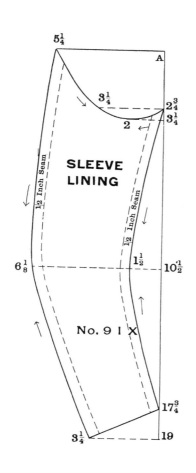

$5\frac{1}{4}$ A

$3\frac{1}{4}$ $2\frac{3}{4}$ $3\frac{1}{4}$

2

SLEEVE
LINING

$1\frac{1}{2}$ Inch Seam $1\frac{1}{2}$ Inch Seam

$6\frac{1}{8}$ $1\frac{1}{2}$ $10\frac{1}{2}$

No. 9 I X

$17\frac{3}{4}$

$3\frac{1}{4}$ 19

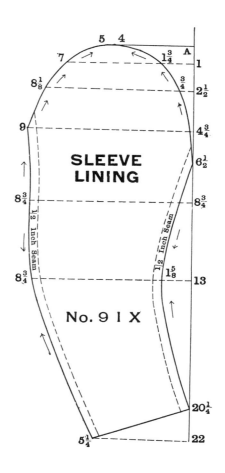

5 4 $1\frac{3}{4}$ A

7 1

$8\frac{1}{8}$ $\frac{3}{4}$ $2\frac{1}{2}$

9 $4\frac{3}{4}$

SLEEVE
LINING $6\frac{1}{2}$

$8\frac{3}{4}$ $8\frac{3}{4}$

$1\frac{1}{2}$ Inch Seam $1\frac{1}{2}$ Inch Seam

$8\frac{3}{4}$ $1\frac{5}{8}$ 13

No. 9 I X

$20\frac{1}{4}$

$5\frac{1}{4}$ 22

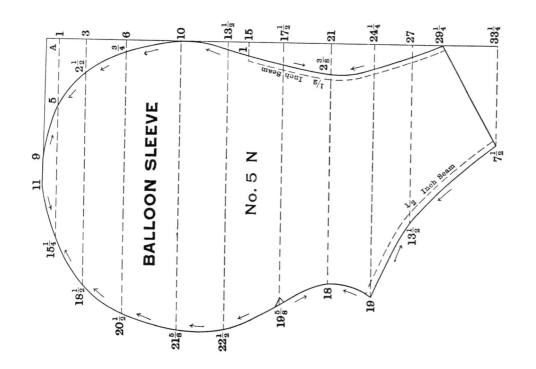

A 1 3 $\frac{3}{4}$ 6 10 $13\frac{1}{2}$ 15 $17\frac{1}{2}$ 21 $24\frac{1}{4}$ 27 $29\frac{1}{4}$ $33\frac{3}{4}$

$2\frac{1}{2}$

5 $2\frac{3}{8}$

1 $1\frac{1}{2}$ Inch Seam

9

BALLOON SLEEVE

11

No. 5 N

$15\frac{1}{4}$

$\frac{1}{2}$ Inch Seam

$18\frac{1}{2}$ $7\frac{1}{2}$

$20\frac{1}{2}$ $13\frac{1}{2}$

$21\frac{5}{8}$ $22\frac{1}{2}$ $19\frac{5}{8}$ 18 19

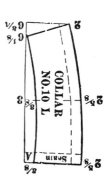

COLLAR
NO.10 L

Spring 1893 / 55

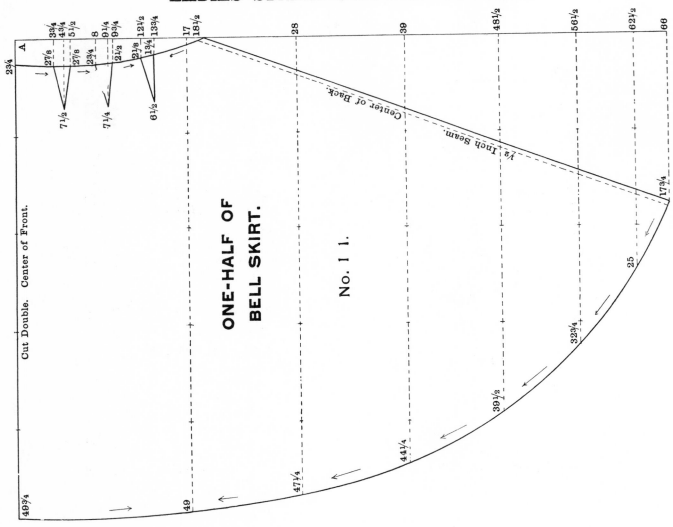

ONE-HALF OF
BELL SKIRT.

No. 11.

Center of Back.

½ Inch Seam.

Cut Double.   Center of Front.

A

LADIES' STREET COSTUME.

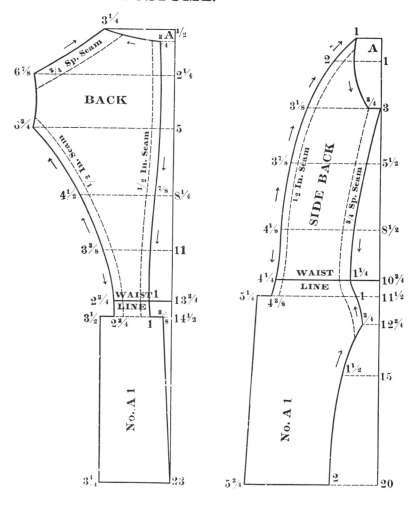

Use the scale corresponding with the Bust Measure to draft the entire Basque and Jacket. The Basque is given on page 57. It consists of Front, Back, Side-back and Under-arm-gore. This is a perfectly plain waist, with a coat-tail back. The upper portions of the front may be turned back to form revers, and a full pointed vest inserted, which always makes a pretty finish to the front. The sleeves are given on page 59.

The Jacket is given on page 58. It consists of Front, Back, Collar and Two Sleeve Portions. This is a half-fitting Jacket. Leave the seams open from the notches down. If made of very light weight goods, line it with silk or silkaline. The collar is given on page 59.

The skirt is given on page 59. Draft by the waist measure. Trim to suit. Regulate length by the tape measure.

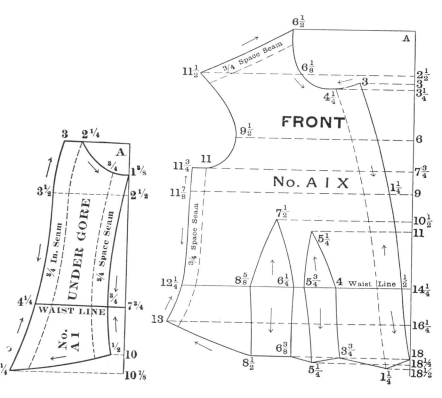

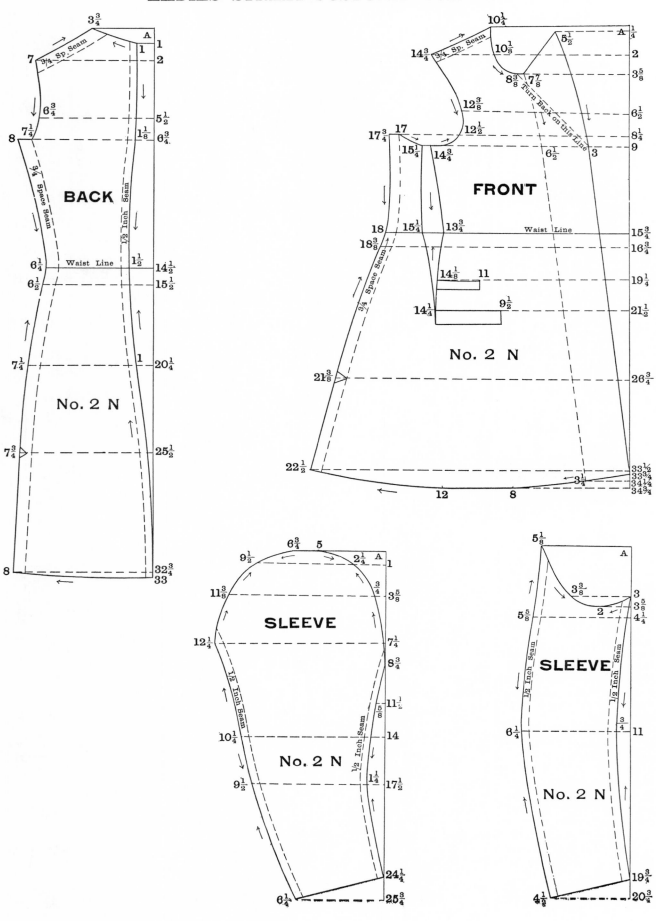

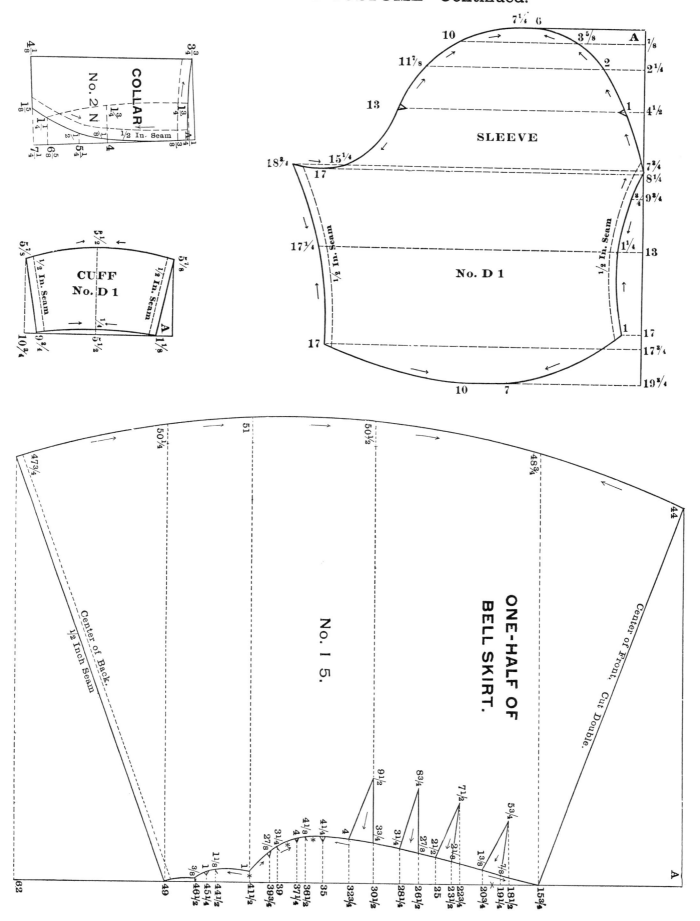

LADIES' RECEPTION GOWN.

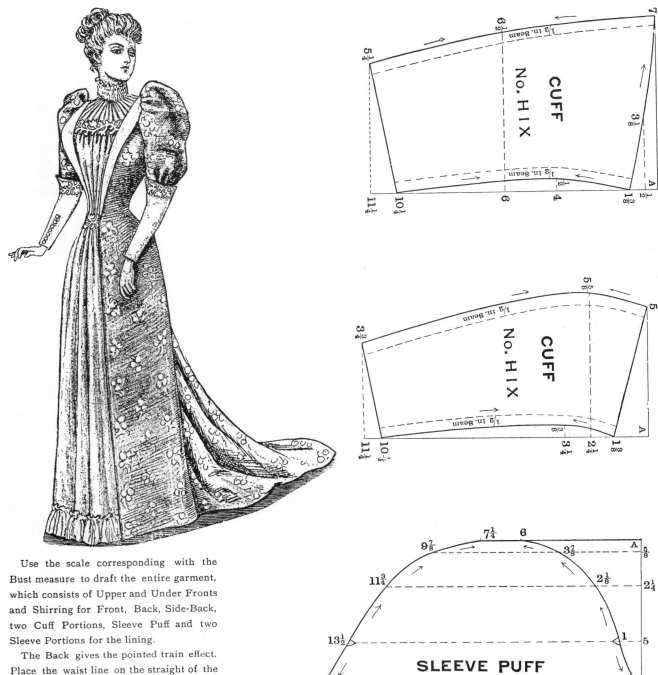

Use the scale corresponding with the Bust measure to draft the entire garment, which consists of Upper and Under Fronts and Shirring for Front, Back, Side-Back, two Cuff Portions, Sleeve Puff and two Sleeve Portions for the lining.

The Back gives the pointed train effect. Place the waist line on the straight of the goods. Shirr the portions given for that purpose and join in the under-arm dart. Fasten at the waist and just over the bust with jeweled embroidery, also trim the deep sleeve cuffs with the same Finish the inside of the cuff with fancy buttons. Gather the puff at the top and bottom and fasten to the lining. Finish the bottom with a band and let the cuffs come over it. Fit the cuff very closely at the wrist.

This Sleeve is suitable for almost any garment except an outside wrap.

Regulate the length by the tape measure.

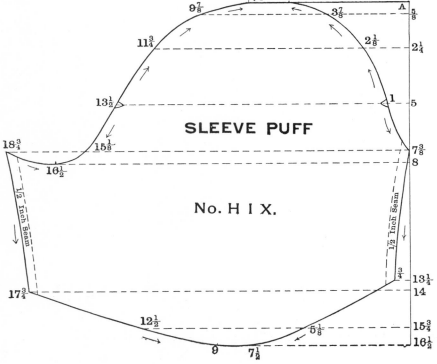

LADIES' RECEPTION GOWN—Continued.

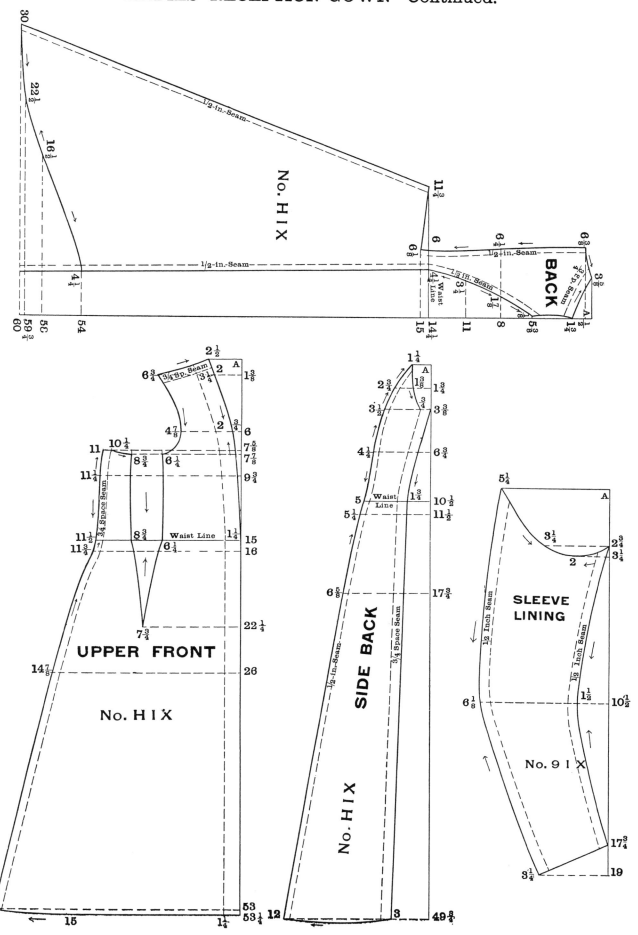

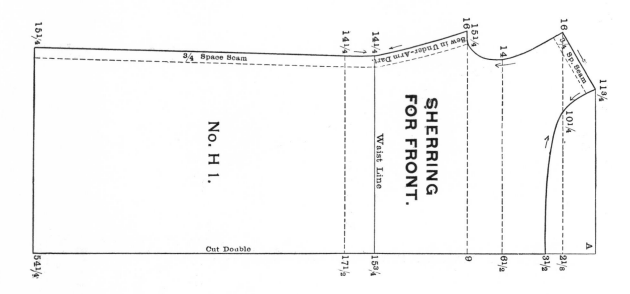

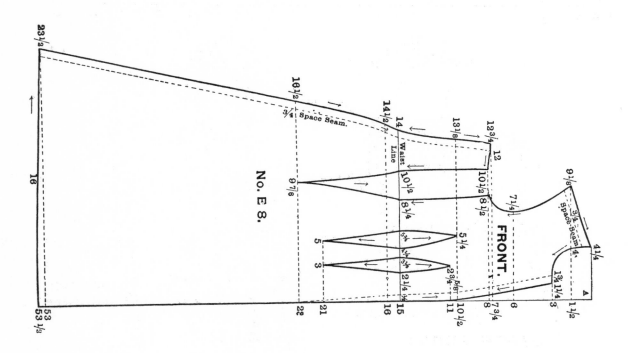

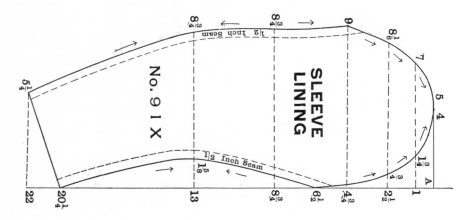

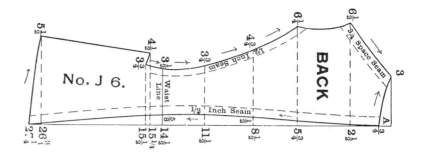

No. J 6.

BACK

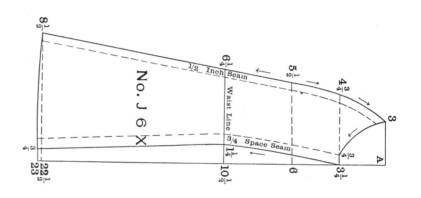

No. J 6 X

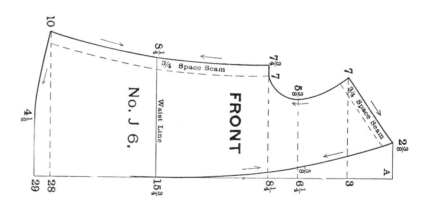

No. J 6.

FRONT

Use the scale corresponding with the Bust measure to draft the entire Waist and Jacket. The Jacket is given on page 63. It consists of Front, Back, Side-Back and Three Sleeve Portions. Line the Jacket with silk. Gather the lower portion of the full sleeve and sew it to the lining. Gather the top between notches.

The Waist is given on page 65. Gather the upper parts and sew to the yoke. Gather the bottoms and sew to a belt. The Under Waist or Lining is given on page 64.

The skirt is given on page 65. Draft by the waist measure. It is simply a straight piece of goods, the length and width required.

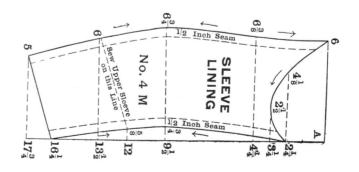

No. 4 M

SLEEVE LINING

Sew Upper Sleeve on this Line

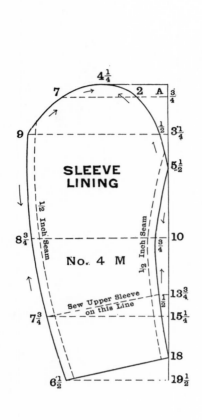

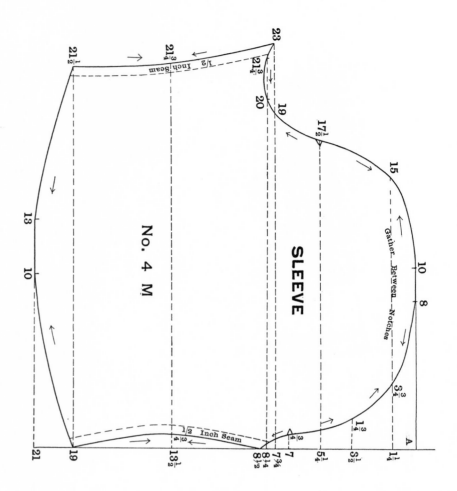

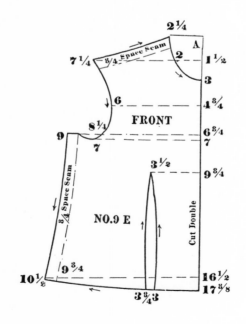

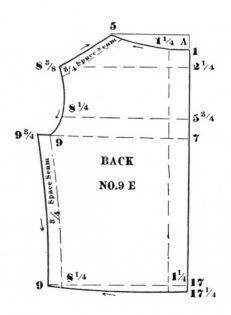

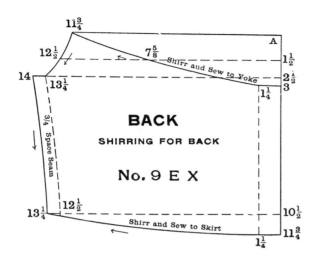

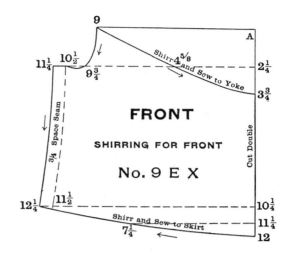

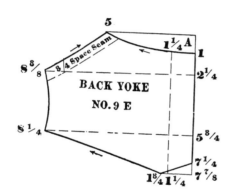

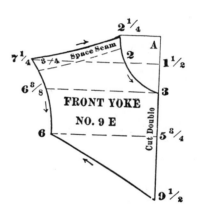

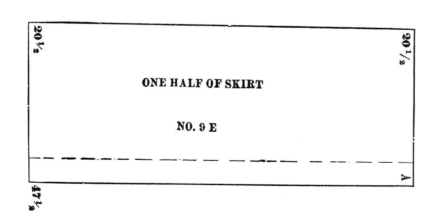

LADIES' STREET COSTUME.

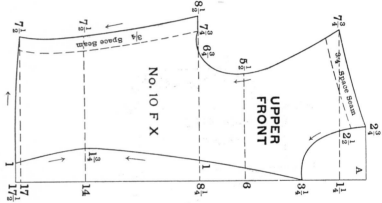

Use the scale corresponding with the Bust measure to draft the entire waist, which consists of Two Fronts, Back, Side-Back, Collar, Full Front and Three Sleeve Portions. Cut the Back double, gather the full front, sew it to the Under-front or lining on the right side. Fasten on the left side with hooks and eyes. The Upper-fronts should be fastened invisibly.

The skirt is given on page 68. Draft by the scale corresponding with the Waist measure. This is one of the new style skirts that gives the full effect below the knee. The top may be gathered if desirable. The darts do away with the fullness at the waist. Any style of trimming may be used. The velvet bands or folds are very pretty. Another pretty way of trimming these skirts is to trim with gathered ruffles half way to the waist, making them four or six inches apart. Face the bottom with canvas or stiff crinoline nearly to the knee, to make it flare out. Regulate the length by the tape measure.

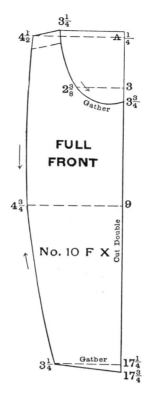

FULL FRONT

No. 10 F X

Cut Double

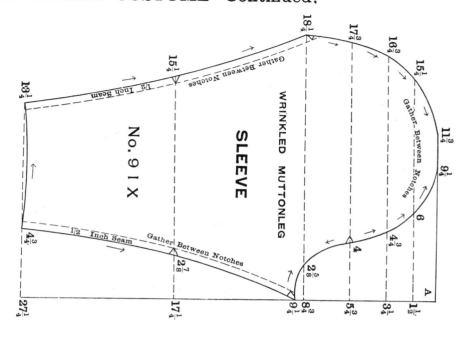

No. 91 X

WRINKLED MUTTONLEG

SLEEVE

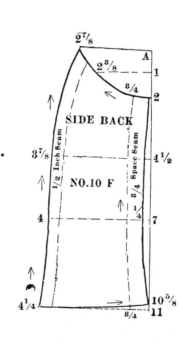

SIDE BACK

NO. 10 F

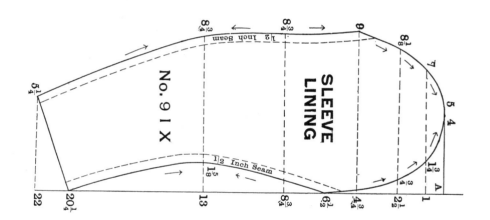

No. 91 X

SLEEVE LINING

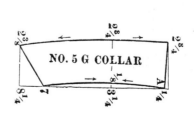

NO. 5 G COLLAR

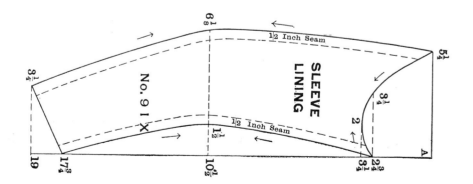

No. 91 X

SLEEVE LINING

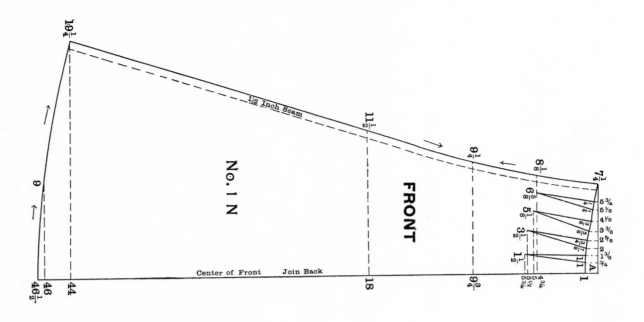

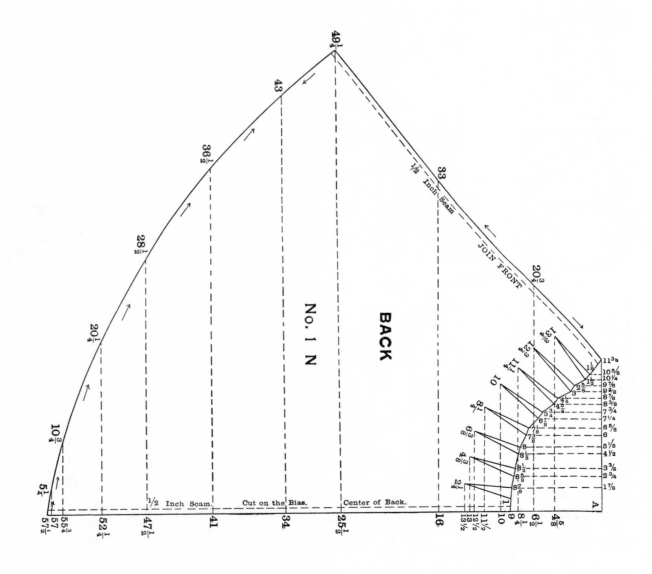

CHILD'S BLOUSE COSTUME.

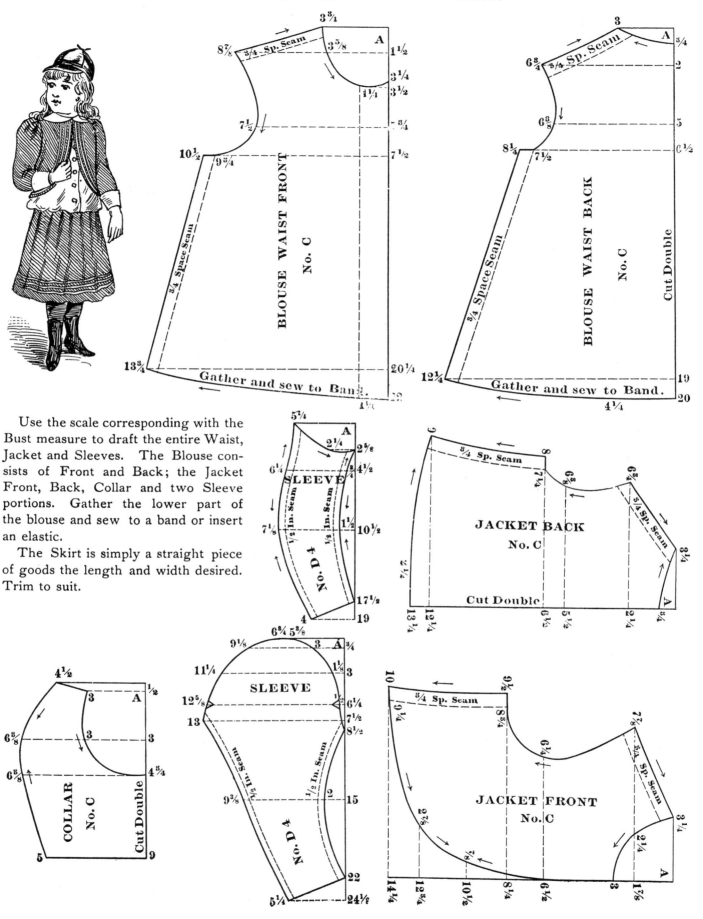

Use the scale corresponding with the Bust measure to draft the entire Waist, Jacket and Sleeves. The Blouse consists of Front and Back; the Jacket Front, Back, Collar and two Sleeve portions. Gather the lower part of the blouse and sew to a band or insert an elastic.

The Skirt is simply a straight piece of goods the length and width desired. Trim to suit.

LADIES' MORNING GOWN

Use the scale corrresponding with the Bust measure to draft the waist and sleeves, which consists of Front, Back and Sleeve. Gather the neck to suit; the waist may be gathered also if desired; if so stitch a piece of cloth on the wrong side to keep it in place; the sleeves are faced up to the second line; shirr to fit the hand; stay it underneath.

Draft the skirt by the waist measure; is in two pieces, Front and Back; take up the darts in front; gather the back; trim to suit.

Regulate the length by the tape-measure.

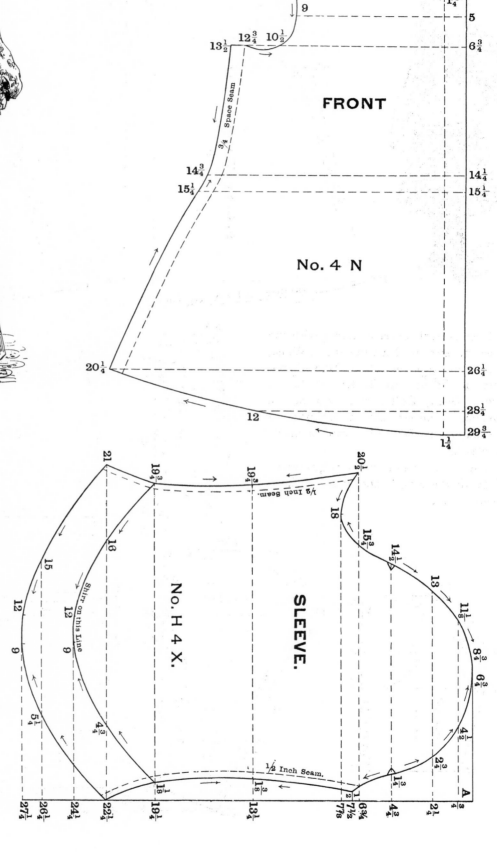

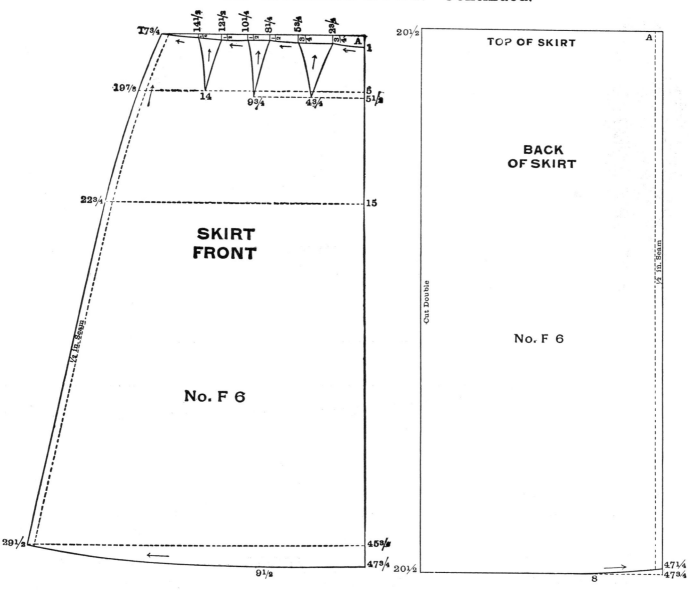

SKIRT FRONT

No. F 6

TOP OF SKIRT

BACK OF SKIRT

No. F 6

Cut Double

½ in. Seam

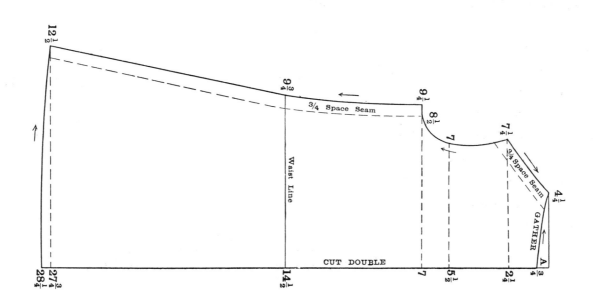

Waist Line

CUT DOUBLE

¾ Space Seam

¾ Space Seam

GATHER

BOY'S SUIT.

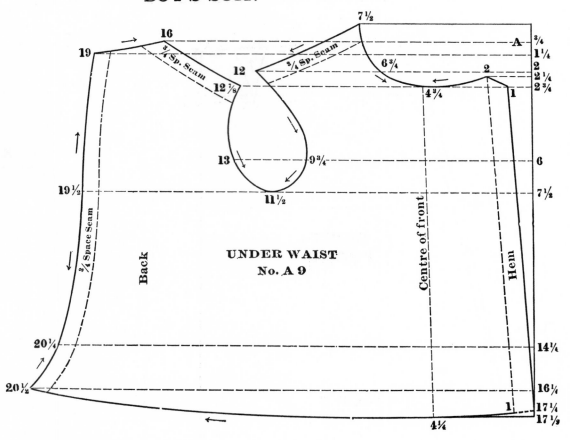

Back

Centre of front

Hem

UNDER WAIST
No. A 9

Use the scale corresponding with the chest measure to draft the under-waist and jacket. The jacket consists of Front, Back, Collar and two Sleeve portions. Draft the same as all other garments. Trim the front on the dotted line to imitate a coat and vest.

Draft the pants by the hip measure; they are given on page 73—front, back, waistband and fly. Take measures from outside or inseam; may be made long or knee pants.

Regulate the length with the tape measure.

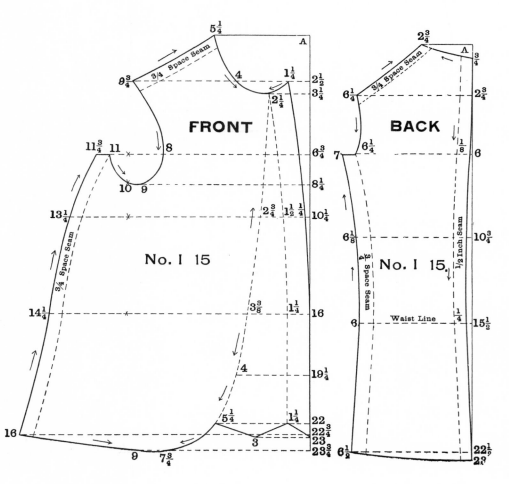

FRONT

No. I 15

BACK

No. I 15.

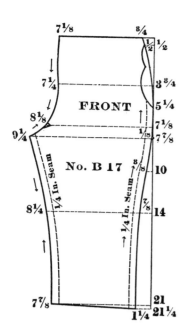

FRONT

No. B 17

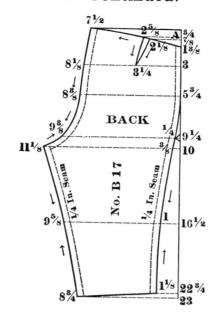

BACK

No. B 17

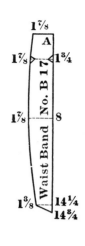

Waist Band No. B 17

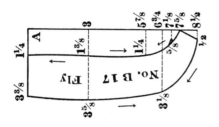

Fly No. B 17

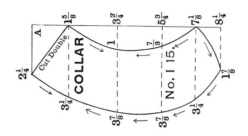

COLLAR No. I 15

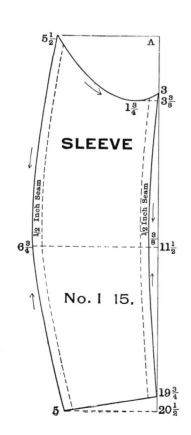

SLEEVE

No. I 15.

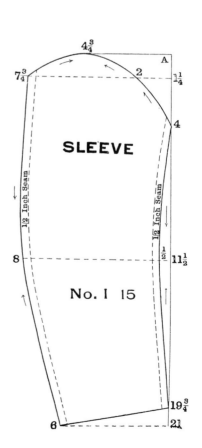

SLEEVE

No. I 15

MISSES' EMPIRE GOWN.

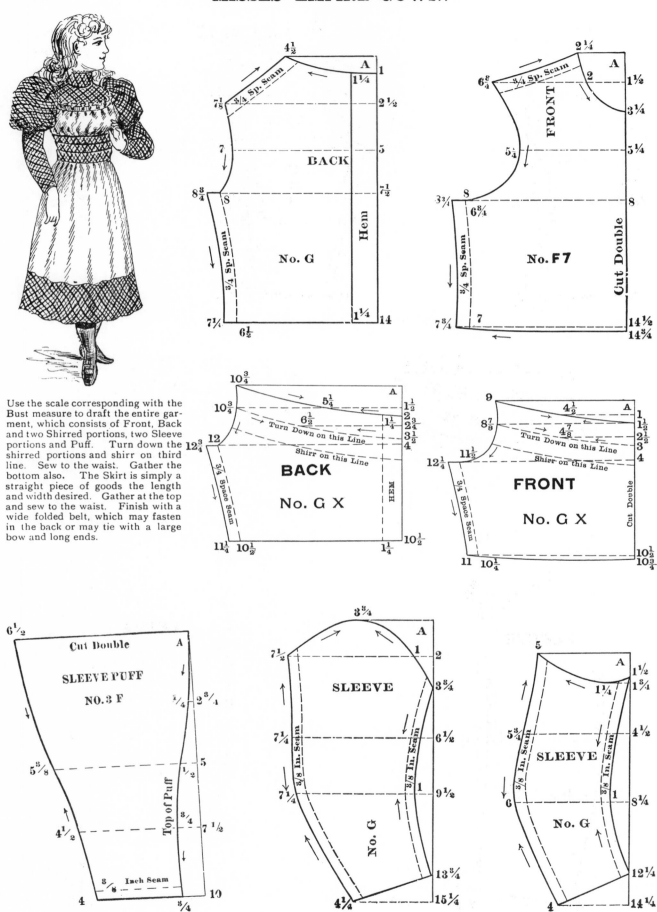

Use the scale corresponding with the Bust measure to draft the entire garment, which consists of Front, Back and two Shirred portions, two Sleeve portions and Puff. Turn down the shirred portions and shirr on third line. Sew to the waist. Gather the bottom also. The Skirt is simply a straight piece of goods the length and width desired. Gather at the top and sew to the waist. Finish with a wide folded belt, which may fasten in the back or may tie with a large bow and long ends.

LADIES' COSTUME.

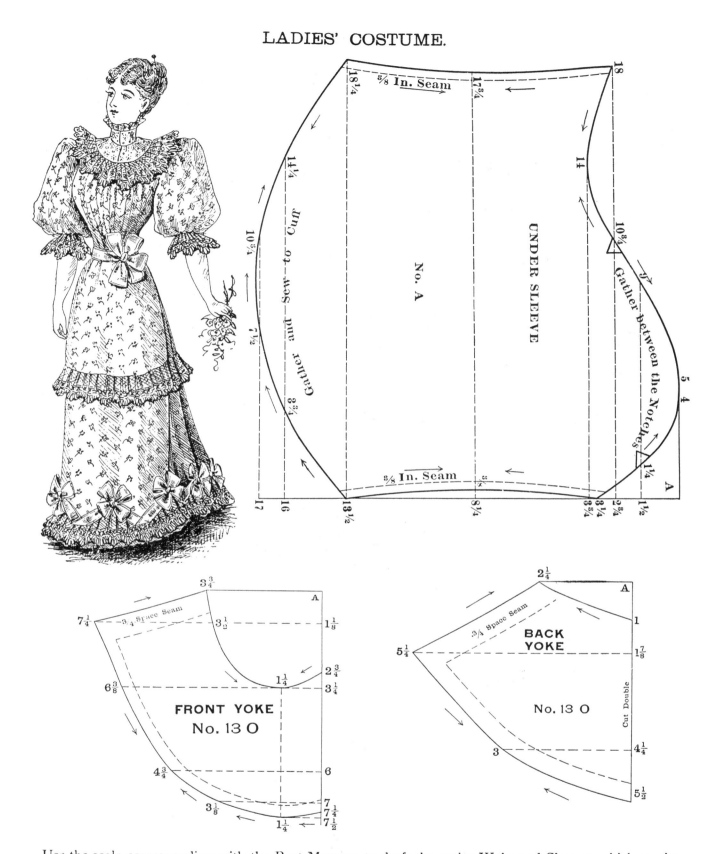

Use the scale corresponding with the Bust Measure to draft the entire Waist and Sleeves, which consist of Front and Front Yoke, Back and Back Yoke, Collar and Sleeve. This gives the round Yoke effect which is very becoming to slender forms. Stout forms should always wear pointed Yokes and Waists.

The Skirt is drafted by the scale corresponding with the Waist Measure. This is what is called the seven gore skirt. Each piece is marked where it joins. Gather the extra fullness at the top and sew to the band, allowing it to fall easy all around. Make it clear the floor. Trim to suit. Regulate the length by the tape-measure.

LADIES' COSTUME—Continued.

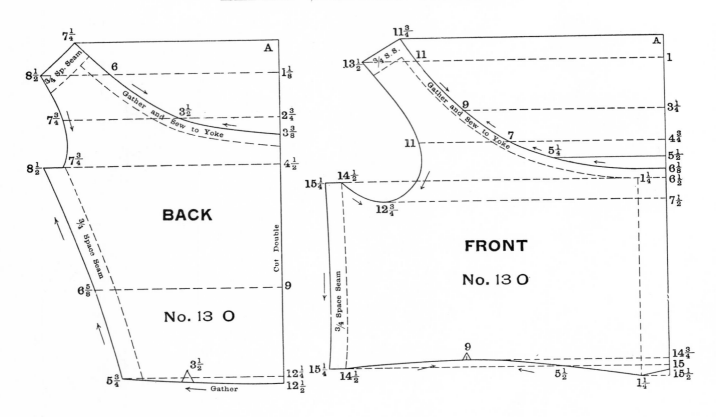

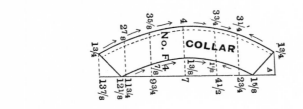

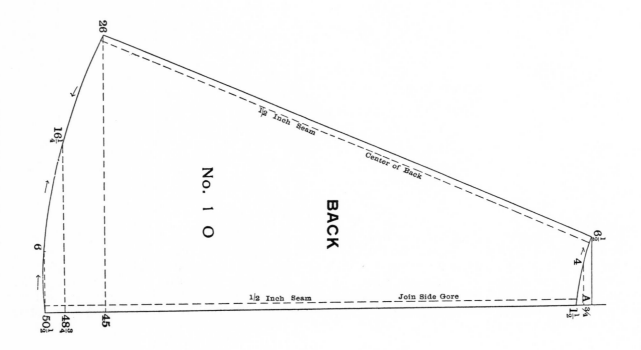

LADIES' COSTUME—Continued.

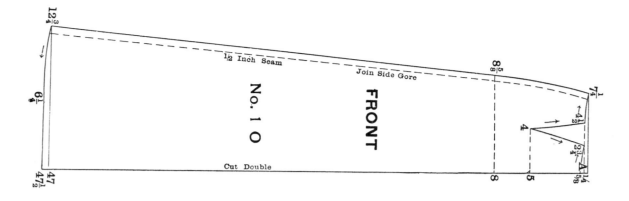

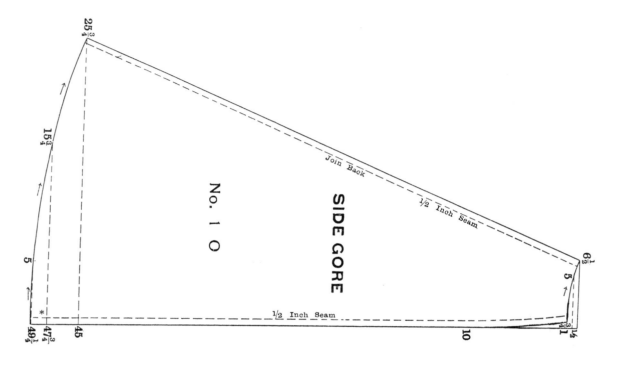

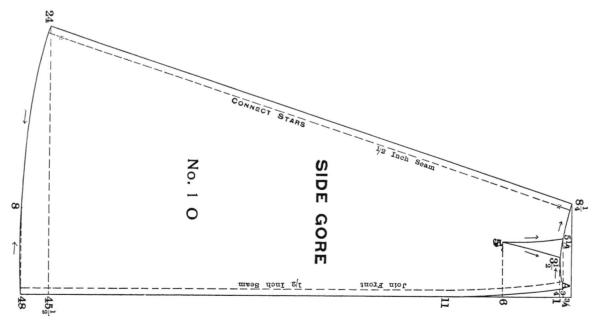

CHILD'S EMPIRE DRESS.

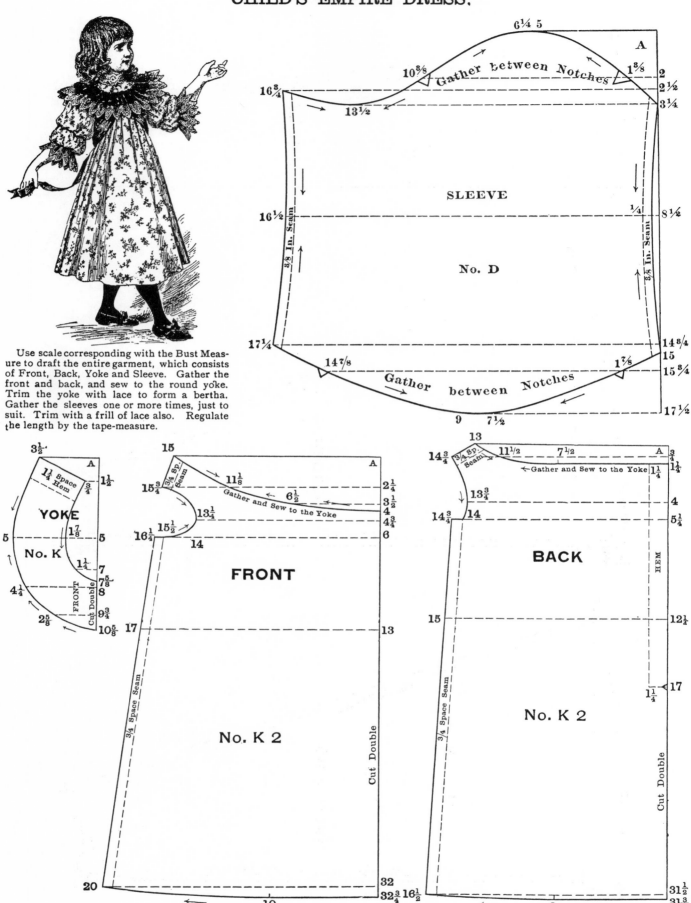

Use scale corresponding with the Bust Measure to draft the entire garment, which consists of Front, Back, Yoke and Sleeve. Gather the front and back, and sew to the round yoke. Trim the yoke with lace to form a bertha. Gather the sleeves one or more times, just to suit. Trim with a frill of lace also. Regulate the length by the tape-measure.

STOUT LADIES' COSTUME.

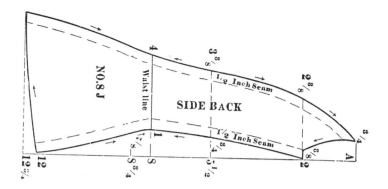

NO.8 J

Waist line

1/2 Inch Seam

SIDE BACK

1/2 Inch Seam

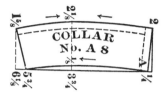

COLLAR
No. A 8

Use the scale corresponding with the Bust Measure to draft the entire Waist and Sleeves, which consist of Front, Back, Side-Back, two under arm Gores, Collar and two Sleeve Portions. Do not use this for a Bust less than 36 inches. It is especially for stout forms. This is a straight round Basque, but can be shaped to suit the wearer. Gather the Sleeve at the top, bring most of the fullness at the sides to make it droop over the arm. Any style of decoration may be used, but flat trimmings are more becoming to stout forms. The Skirt in given on page 81. Draft by the Waist Measure. If more fullness is desired two side Gores may be cut instead of one. Trim to suit. Regulate the length by the tape measure.

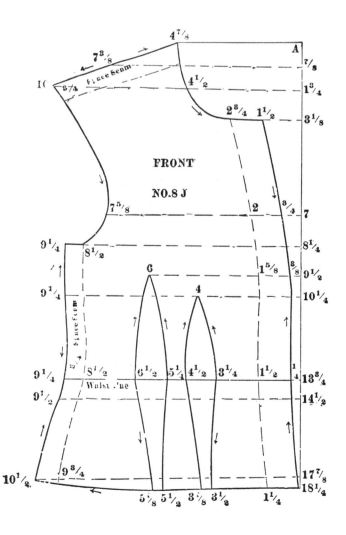

FRONT

NO.8 J

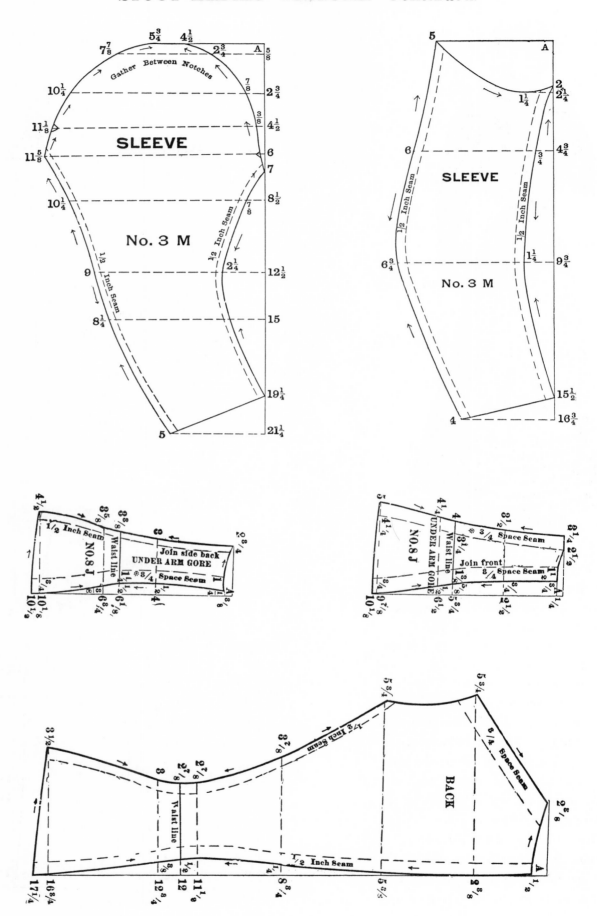

STOUT LADIES' COSTUME—Continued.

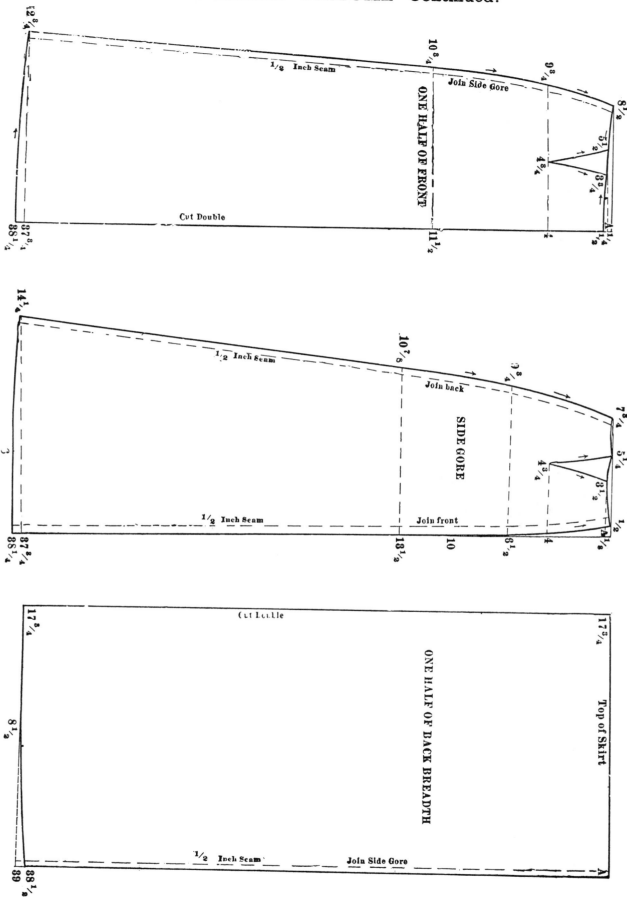

ONE HALF OF FRONT

Join Side Gore

1/2 Inch Seam

Cut Double

SIDE GORE

Join back

Join front

1/2 Inch Seam

1/2 Inch Seam

ONE HALF OF BACK BREADTH

Top of Skirt

Cut Double

1/2 Inch Seam   Join Side Gore

LADIES STREET COSTUME.

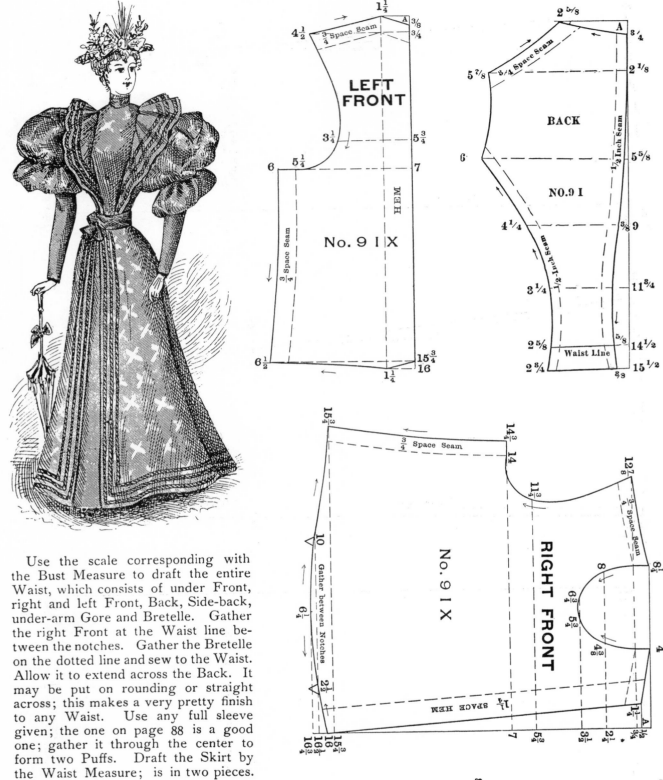

LEFT FRONT

NO. 9 I X

BACK

NO. 9 I

RIGHT FRONT

NO. 9 I X

BRETELLE

NO. 6 O

Use the scale corresponding with the Bust Measure to draft the entire Waist, which consists of under Front, right and left Front, Back, Side-back, under-arm Gore and Bretelle. Gather the right Front at the Waist line between the notches. Gather the Bretelle on the dotted line and sew to the Waist. Allow it to extend across the Back. It may be put on rounding or straight across; this makes a very pretty finish to any Waist. Use any full sleeve given; the one on page 88 is a good one; gather it through the center to form two Puffs. Draft the Skirt by the Waist Measure; is in two pieces. This may be simply trimmed to represent an Overskirt; or cut two Fronts, cut one double down the center, and cut the other open. Trim with folds, velvet or braid. Regulate the length to suit.

LADIES' STREET COSTUME—Continued.

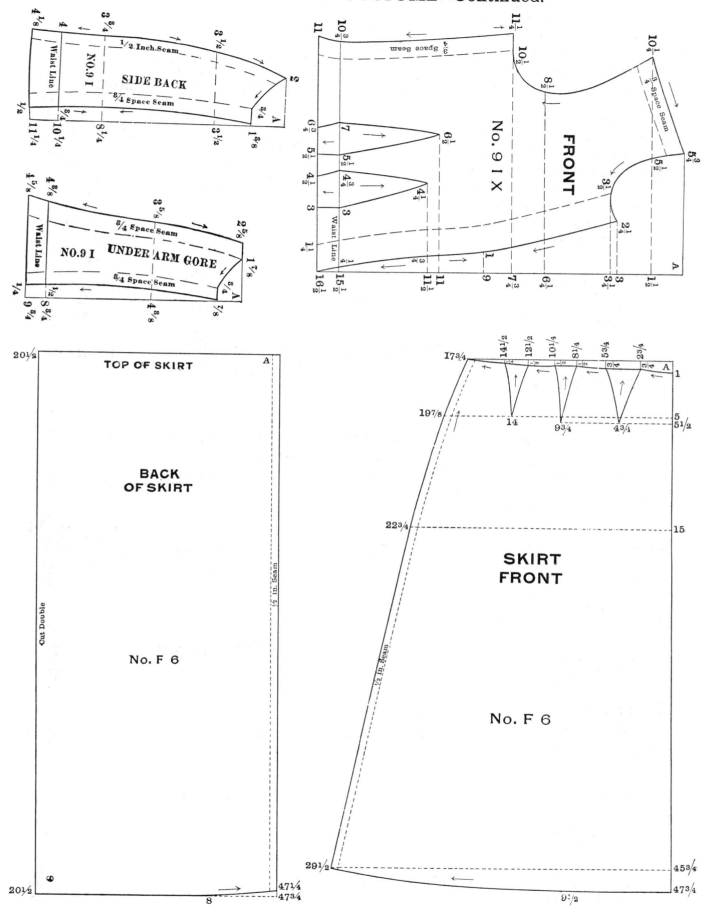

GENTLEMAN'S PRINCE ALBERT COAT.

Use the scale corresponding with Chest measure to draft the entire garment, which consists of Front, Back, Side Back, Lap for the Front, Collar, Coat Skirt and two Sleeve portions.

We also give a work Blouse (by request). Draft by Chest measure; is in five pieces, ½ of Waist, Sleeve, Collar, Yoke and Front Lap. The Yoke extends across the Back and over the Shoulder. The Sleeves for the Coat are given on page 85, also the work Blouse.

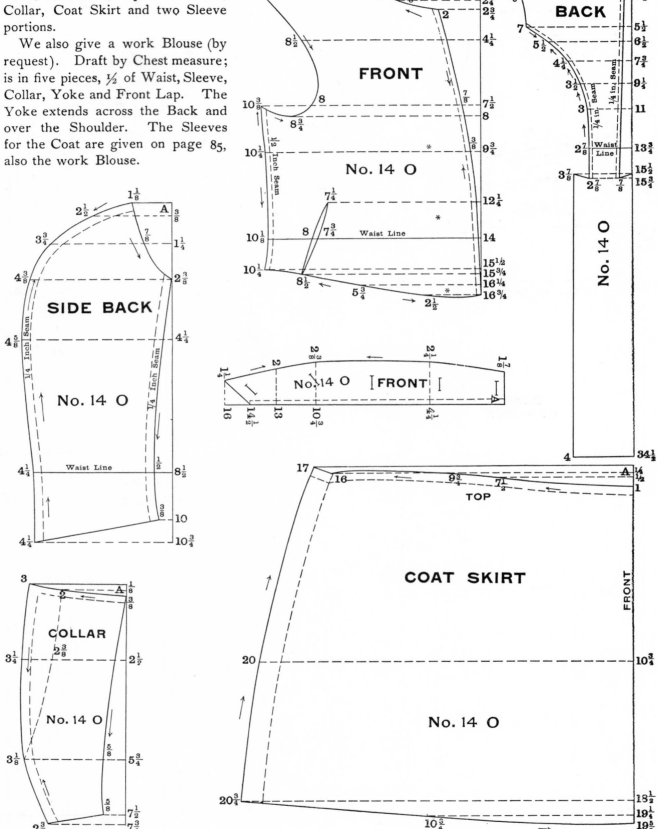

GENTLEMAN'S PRINCE ALBERT COAT—Continued.

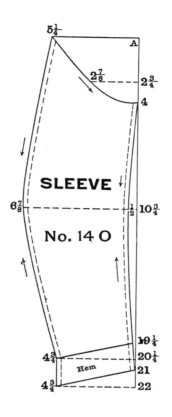

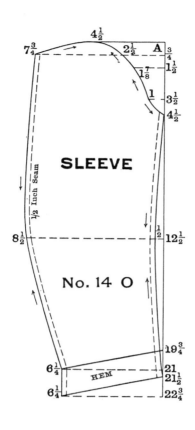

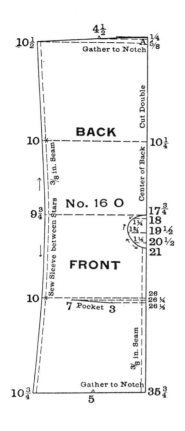

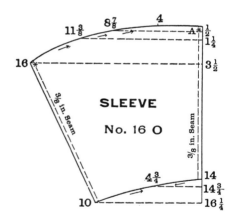

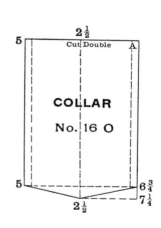

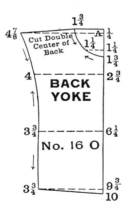

LADIES' STREET COSTUME.

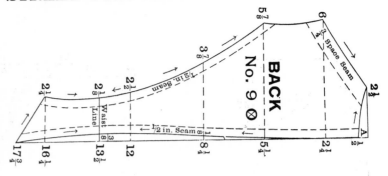

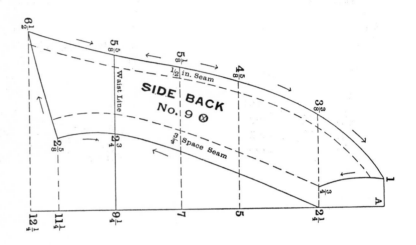

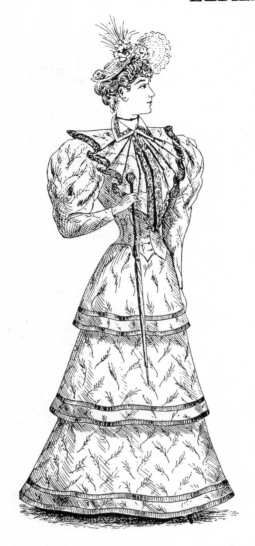

Use scale corresponding with the Bust measure to draft the waist and sleeves, which consists of Front, Back, Side-back, Collar and Sleeve. This is a pointed back and two points in front. Shape the bottom to suit. The sleeve is gathered between notches, over the top and down the sides. Lay the pleats in the Derby Cape according to the notches. Line with contrasting material.

The Skirt is given on page 87. Draft by the waist measure, trim with scant deep flounces, or any other style. If the flounces are not used, put in an extra breadth in the center of back to give the required fullness.

Regulate the length by the tape-measure.

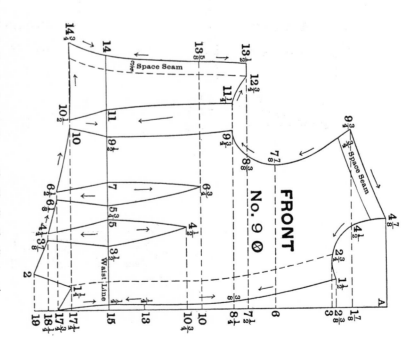

LADIES' STREET COSTUME—Continued.

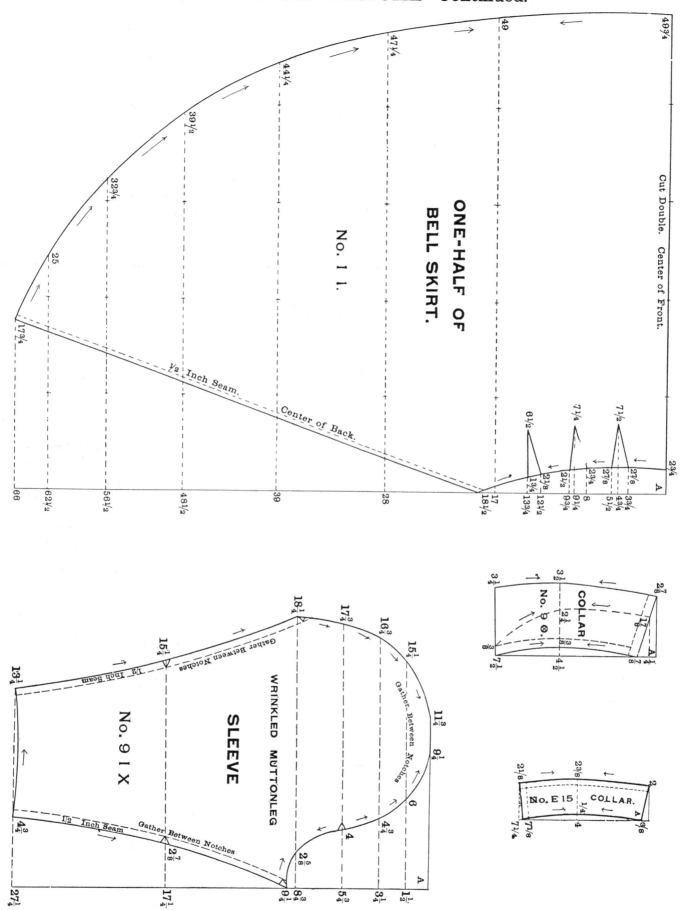

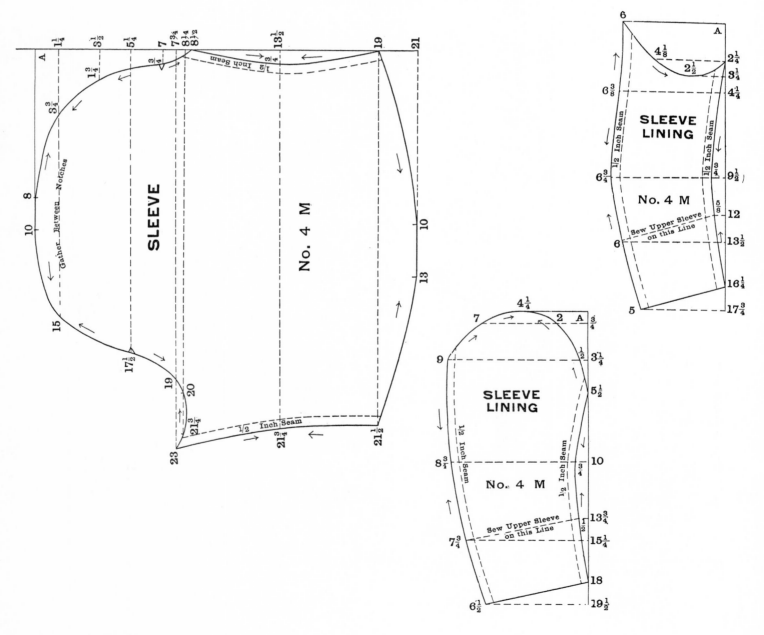

DERBY CAPE

No. 90

LADIES' FULL SLEEVE

SLEEVE

No. 4 M

SLEEVE LINING

No. 4 M

SLEEVE LINING

No. 4 M

LADIES' STREET COSTUME.

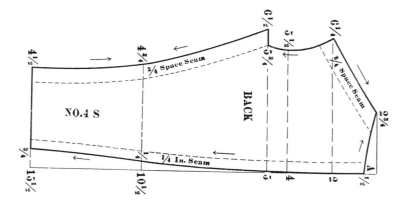

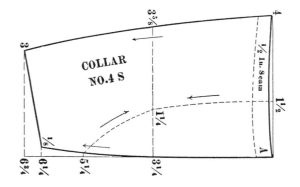

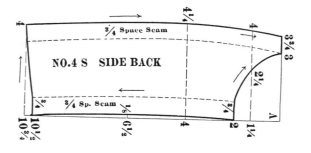

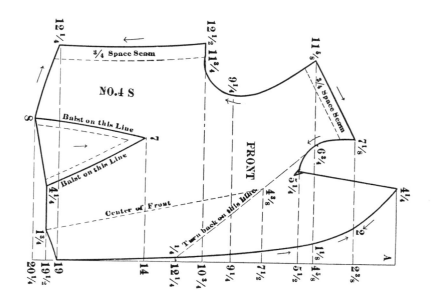

Use the scale corresponding with the Bust measure to draft the entire Basque, which consists of Front, Back, Sideback, Collar, Coat or (Basque) Skirt and two Sleeve portions.

Fit the waist perfectly. Lap the fronts from right to left. Button or hook down the side. After lining the skirt with silk to make it fall in graceful waves sew to the waist. It may be finished all around with stitching.

The upper sleeve is laid in box pleats according to the notches. The notches represent the pleats, and the stars the under side of the pleat.

The Skirt is given on page 91. Draft by the Waist measure. Is in two pieces—Gored Front and Bell Back. Gather the center of the back from the notch. Regulate the length by the tape measure.

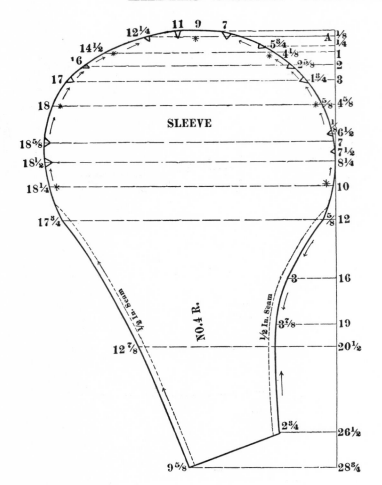

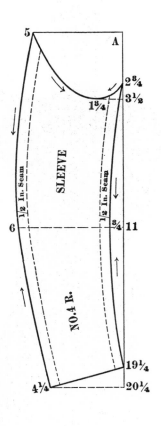

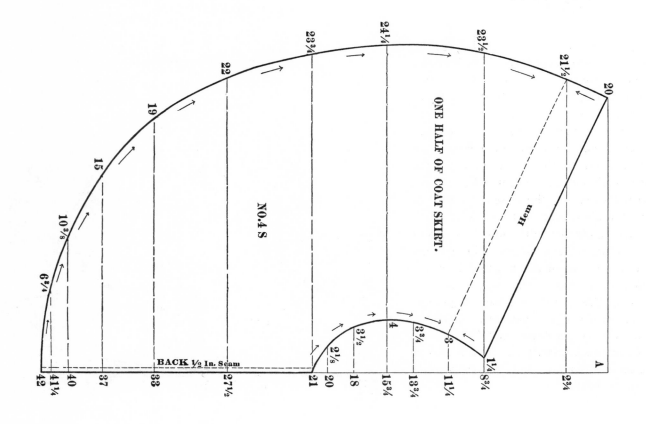

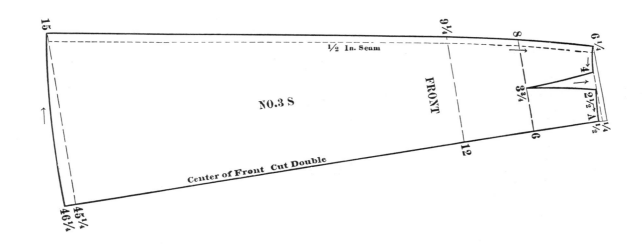

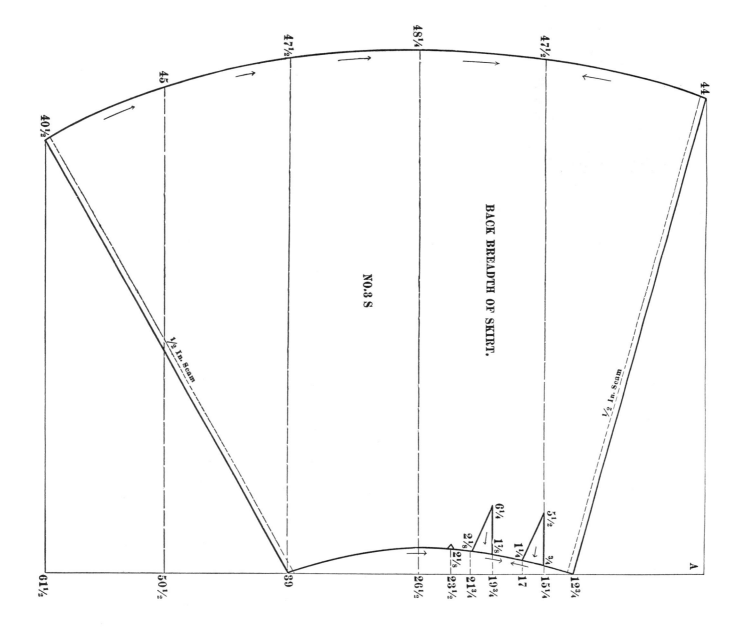

LADIES' PRINCESS GOWN.

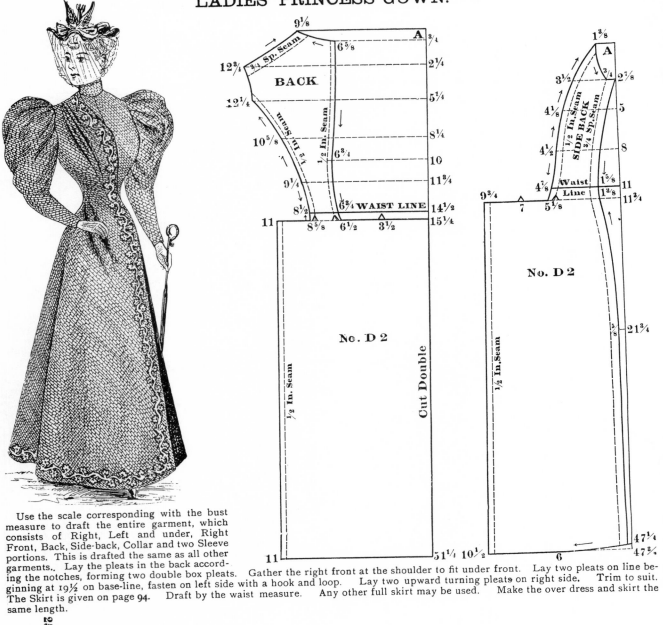

Use the scale corresponding with the bust measure to draft the entire garment, which consists of Right, Left and under, Right Front, Back, Side-back, Collar and two Sleeve portions. This is drafted the same as all other garments.. Lay the pleats in the back according the notches, forming two double box pleats. The Skirt is given on page 94. Draft by the waist measure.

Gather the right front at the shoulder to fit under front. Lay two pleats on line beginning at 19½ on base-line, fasten on left side with a hook and loop. Lay two upward turning pleats on right side. Trim to suit. Any other full skirt may be used. Make the over dress and skirt the same length.

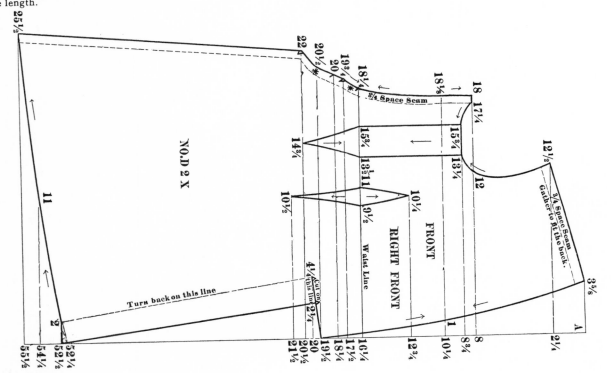

LADIES' PRINCESS GOWN—Continued.

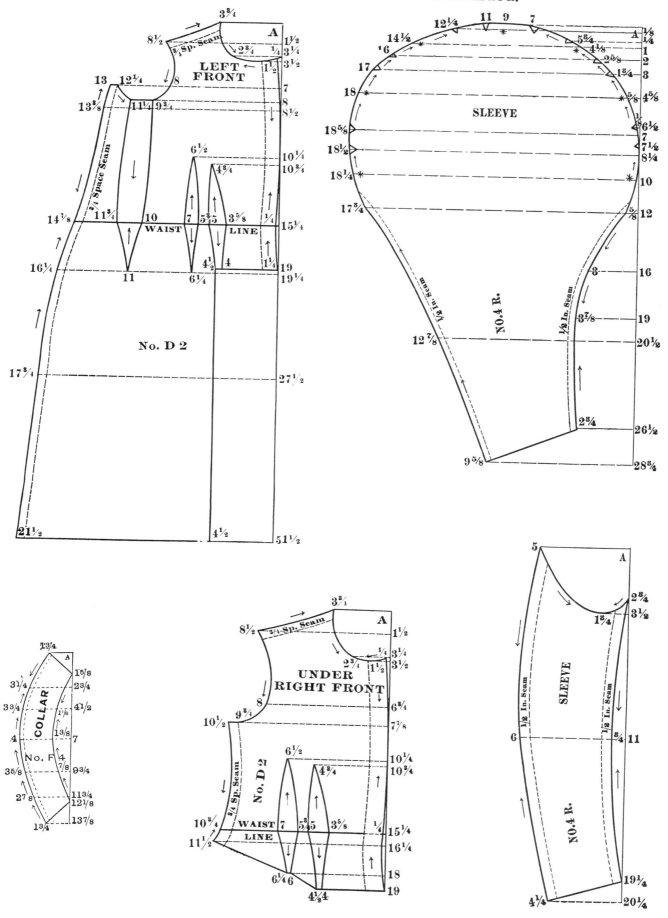

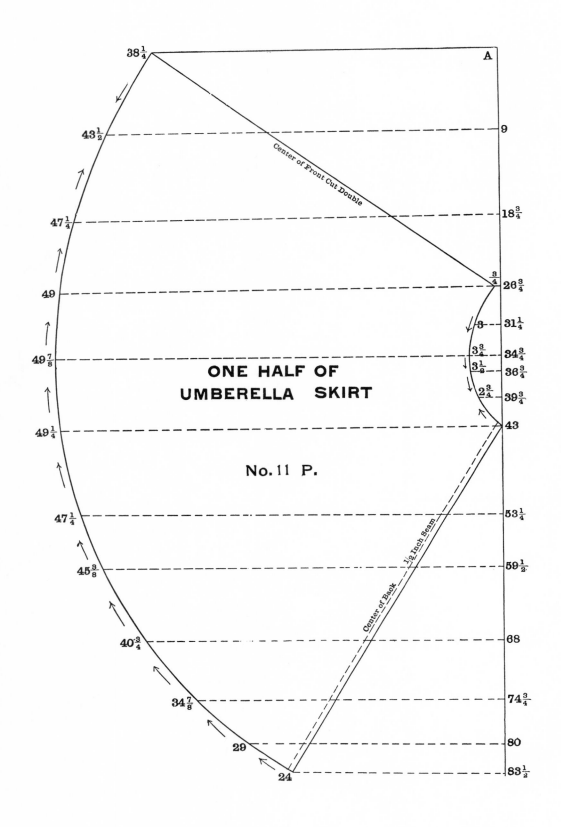

38¼

A

43½ — — — — — — — — — — — — — — — — 9

Center of Front Cut Double

47¼ — — — — — — — — — — — — — — — 18¾

49 — — — — — — — — — — — — — — ¾|26¾

3|31¼

ONE HALF OF
UMBERELLA   SKIRT

49⅞ — — — — — — — — — — 3¾|34¾
3½|36¾
2¾|39¾

No. 11 P.

49¼ — — — — — — — — — — — — — 43

47¼ — — — — — — — — — — — — — — 53¼

45⅜ — — — — — — — — — — — — — 59½

Center of Back ½ Inch Seam

40¾ — — — — — — — — — — — — — 68

34⅞ — — — — — — — — — — — — 74¾

29

80

24 — — — — 83½

LADIES' COSTUME.

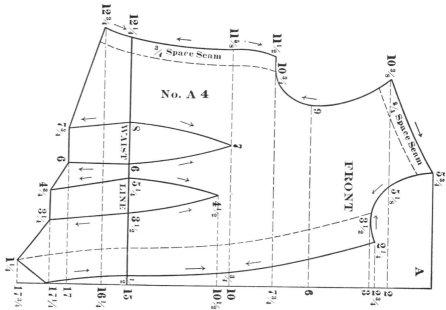

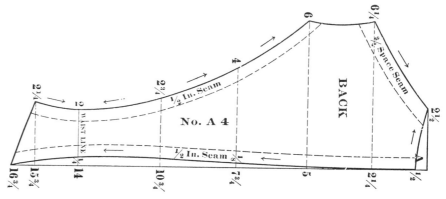

Use the scale corresponding with the bust measure to draft the entire waist and sleeves, which consists of Front, Back, Side-Back, Under-arm-gore, Collar, Bretelle and three Sleeve portions. This basque gives the pointed effect both back and front. Put the parts together as usual. Whalebone every seam. Line the bretelle with soft silk. Gather all around and sew to waist, forming a point both front and back. Gather the balloon sleeve all around the top.

Tho Front of the skirt is given on page 96. The two Side-gores and Back are given on page 97. Draft by the waist measure. Trim to suit.

Regulate the length by the tape measure.

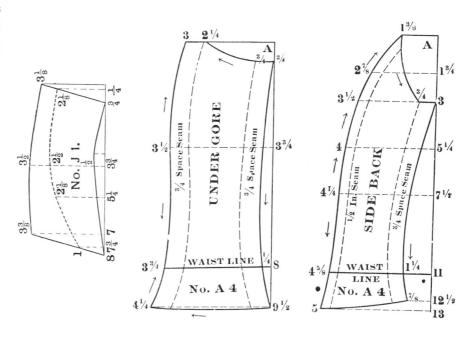

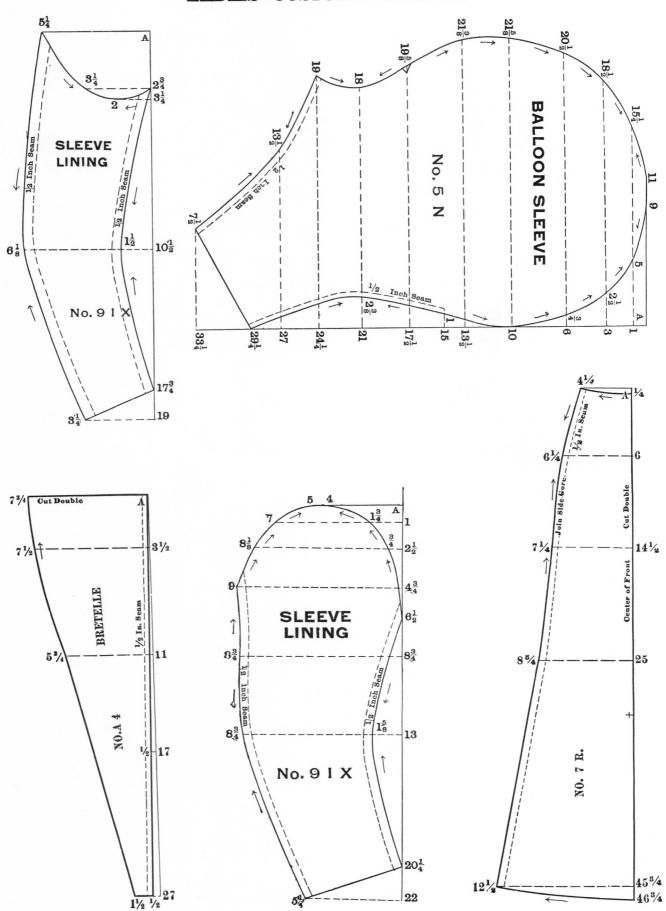

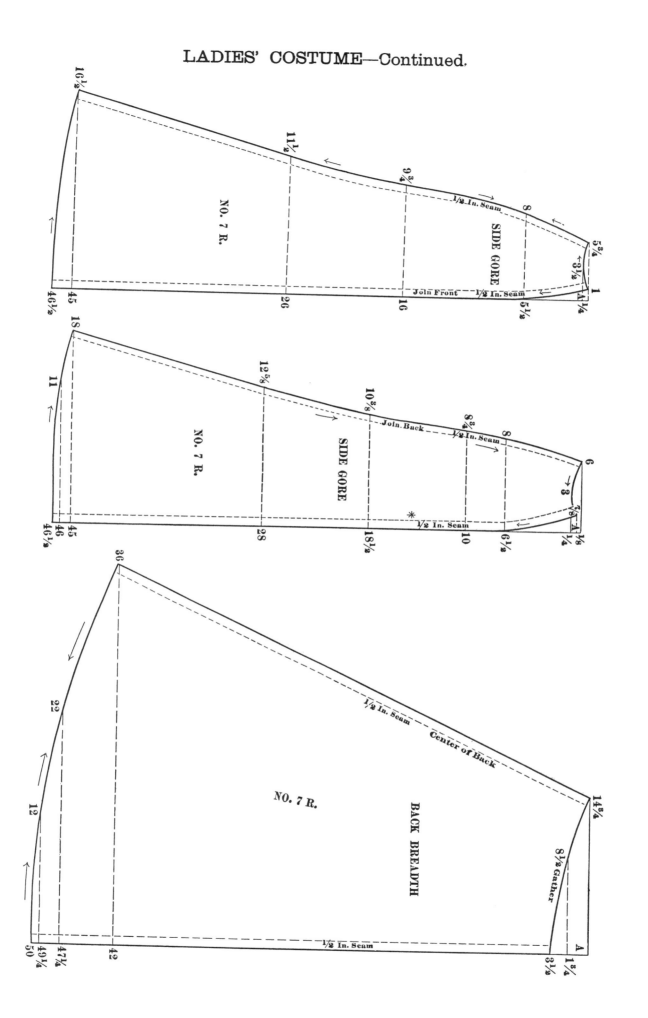

MISSES' COSTUME.

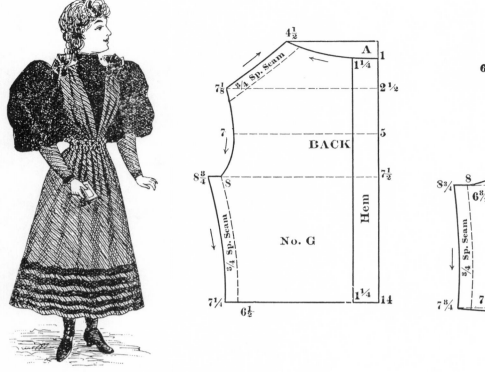

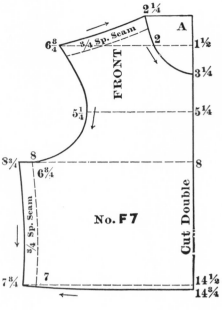

Use the scale corresponding with the bust measure to draft the entire waist and sleeves, which consists of two Fronts, two Backs, Collar and three Sleeve portions. Cut the front double and close in the back. Gather the upper portions at the shoulders and waist line. The upper portions and skirt may be made separate and worn with various waists. Gather the puff for the sleeve and sew on the dotted line, or higher up if a deeper cuff is desired. The Skirt is given on page 99. Draft by the waist measure.

Regulate the length by the tape measure.

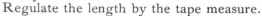

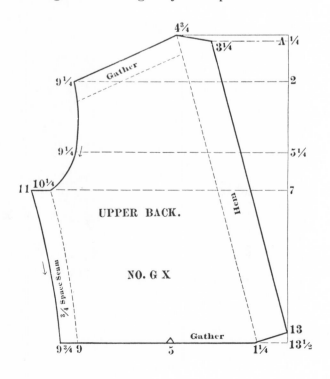

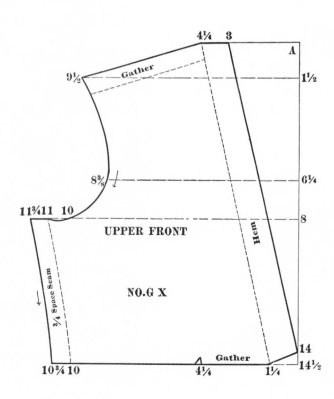

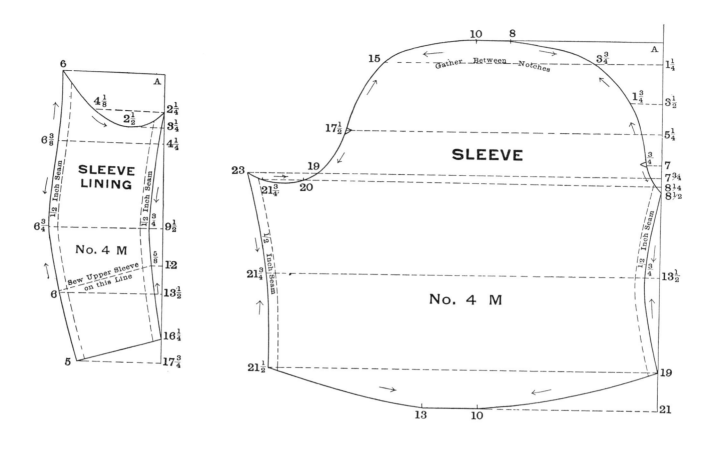

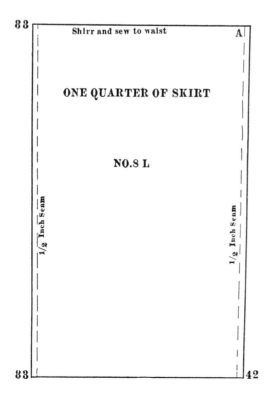

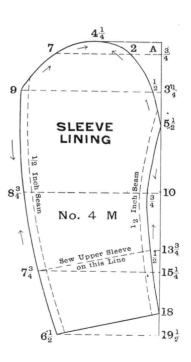

LADIES' HOUSE GOWN.

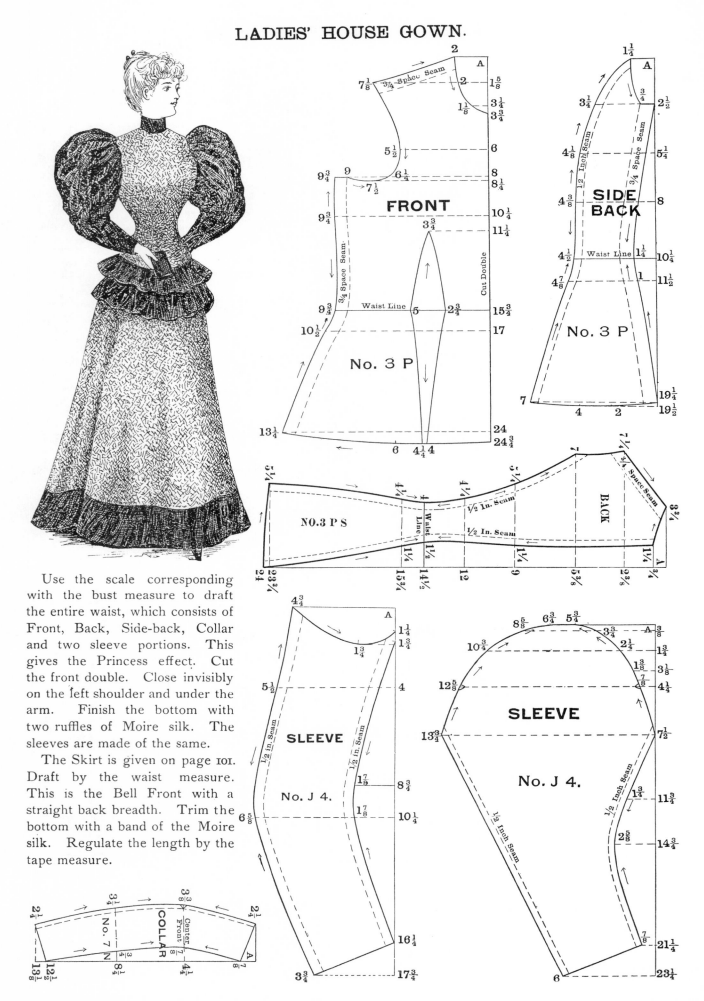

Use the scale corresponding with the bust measure to draft the entire waist, which consists of Front, Back, Side-back, Collar and two sleeve portions. This gives the Princess effect. Cut the front double. Close invisibly on the left shoulder and under the arm. Finish the bottom with two ruffles of Moire silk. The sleeves are made of the same.

The Skirt is given on page 101. Draft by the waist measure. This is the Bell Front with a straight back breadth. Trim the bottom with a band of the Moire silk. Regulate the length by the tape measure.

LADIES' HOUSE GOWN.

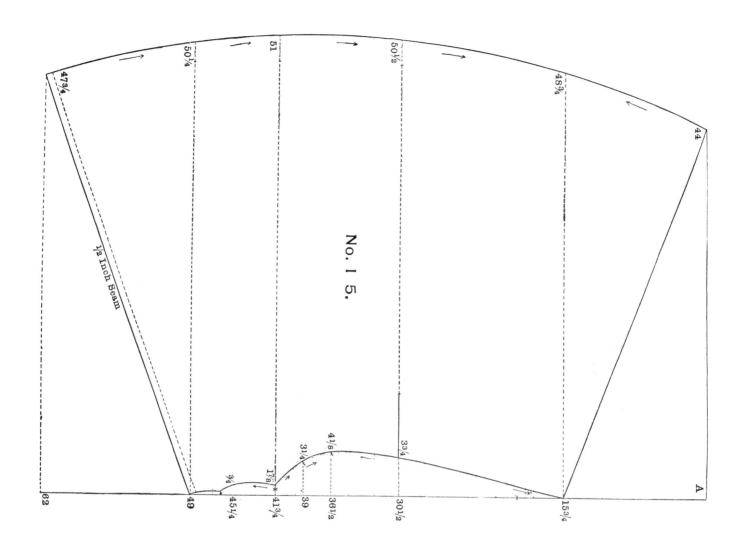

No. 15.

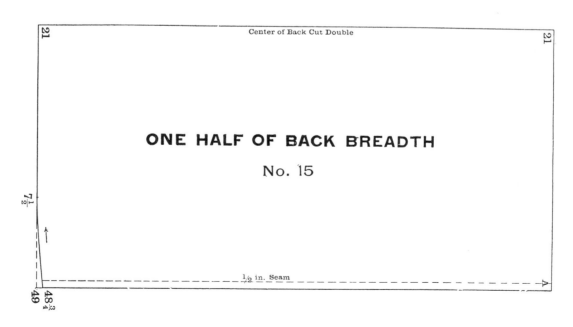

ONE HALF OF BACK BREADTH

No. 15

MISSES' EVENING GOWN.

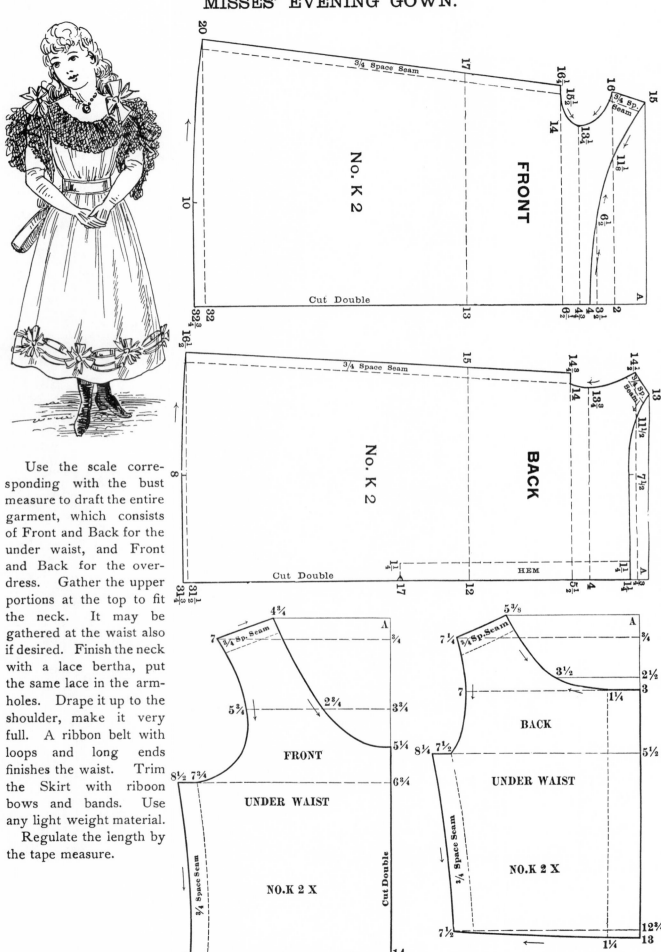

Use the scale corresponding with the bust measure to draft the entire garment, which consists of Front and Back for the under waist, and Front and Back for the overdress. Gather the upper portions at the top to fit the neck. It may be gathered at the waist also if desired. Finish the neck with a lace bertha, put the same lace in the armholes. Drape it up to the shoulder, make it very full. A ribbon belt with loops and long ends finishes the waist. Trim the Skirt with riboon bows and bands. Use any light weight material.

Regulate the length by the tape measure.

LADIES' STREET COSTUME.

Use the scale corresponding with the bust measure to draft the entire waist, jacket and sleeves.

The jacket consists of front, back and side-back, under-arm-gore, collar, and three sleeve portions; draft same as all other garments. Line throughout with silk, fasten on the left shoulder and left side. It is a tight fitting back and half fitting front. Trim with braiding. Lay the sleeve in a triple box pleat.

The waist is given on page 106. Cut the back double, gather at waist line between notches. Pleat the front according to notches, lap across the front, fasten on the side with a belt and rosette. Make of silk or wash goods such as lawns, dimities, mull or swiss. The sleeves for the waist may be made from any sleeve given. The neck and down the front may be finished with lace or fine pleating.

The skirt is given on pages 106 and 107. Draft by the waist measure. It consists of front, two side gores and back breadth. This makes a very full skirt, but that is what the present styles require. Join the different parts as indicated, face the bottom up 13 inches with hair cloth, cross barred crinoline or heavy canvas to make it stand out at the foot. Trim with braiding to correspond with the jacket. Regulate the length by the tape measure.

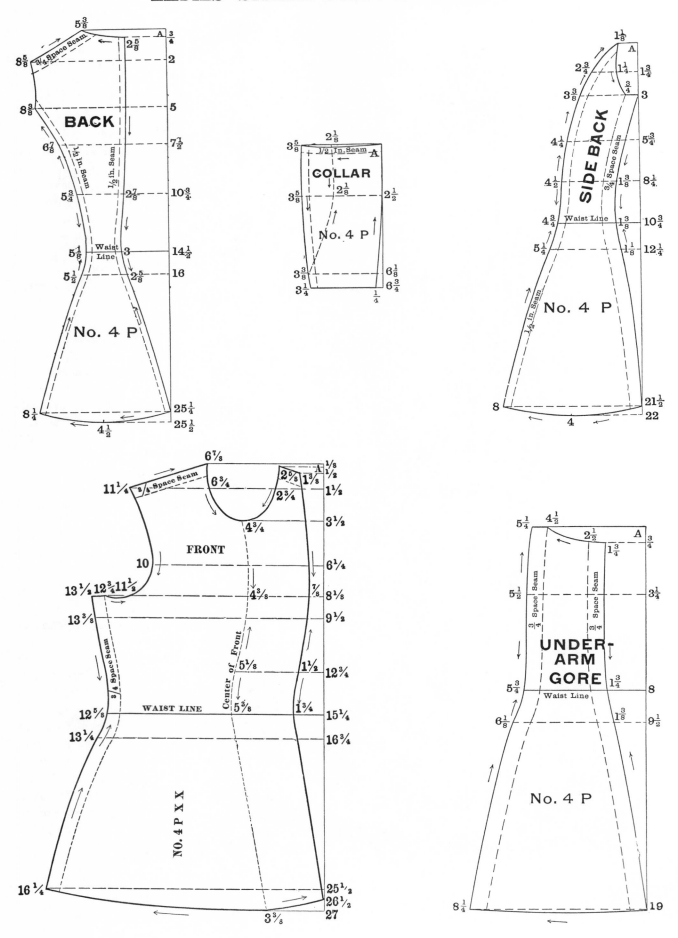

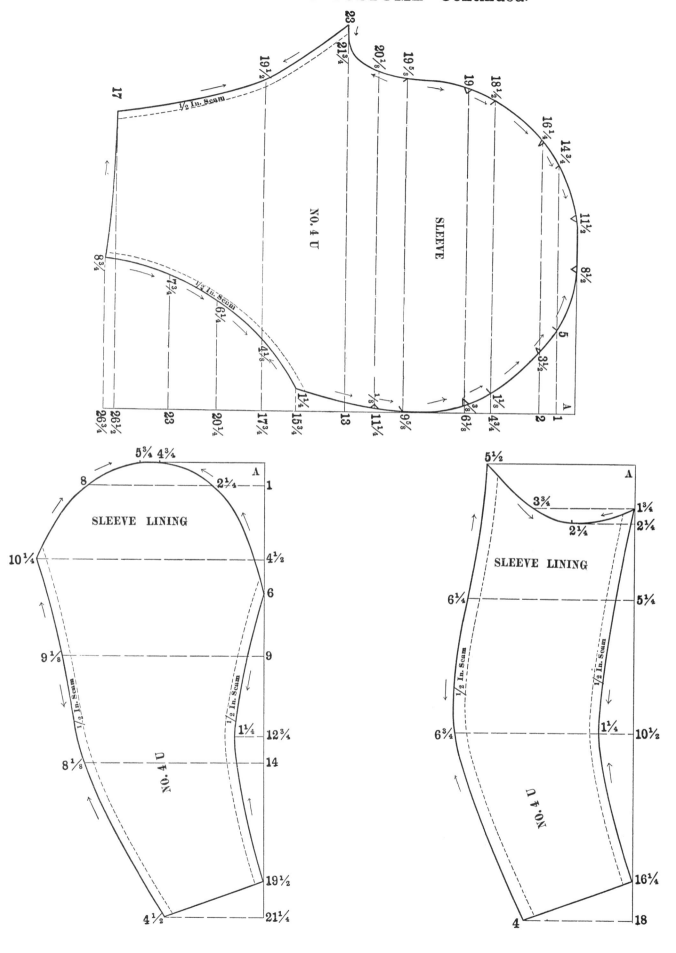

LADIES' STREET COSTUME—Continued.

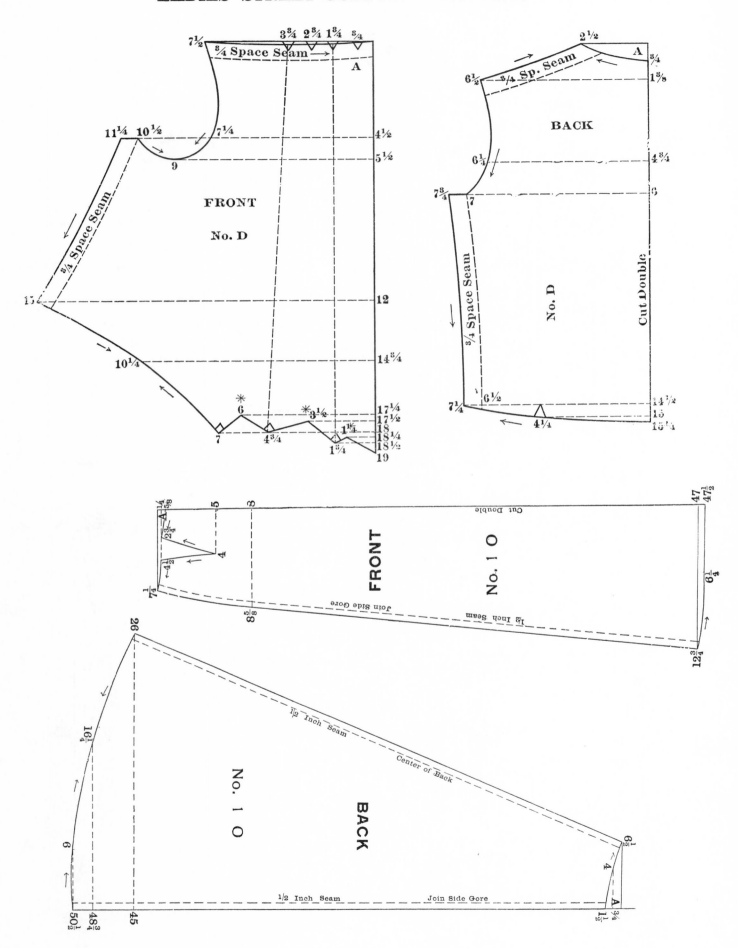

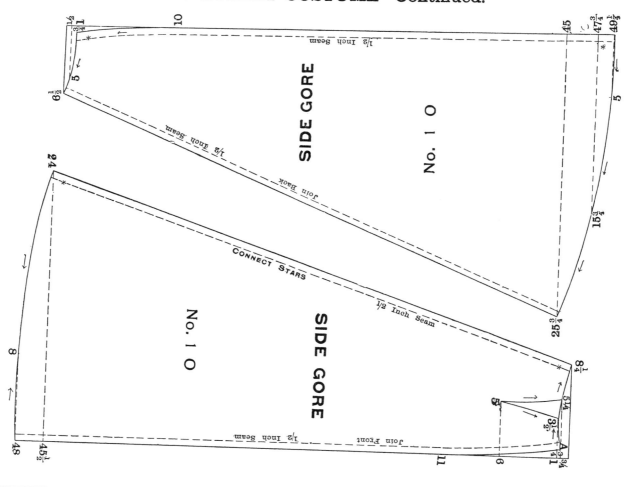

UMBRELLA SKIRT

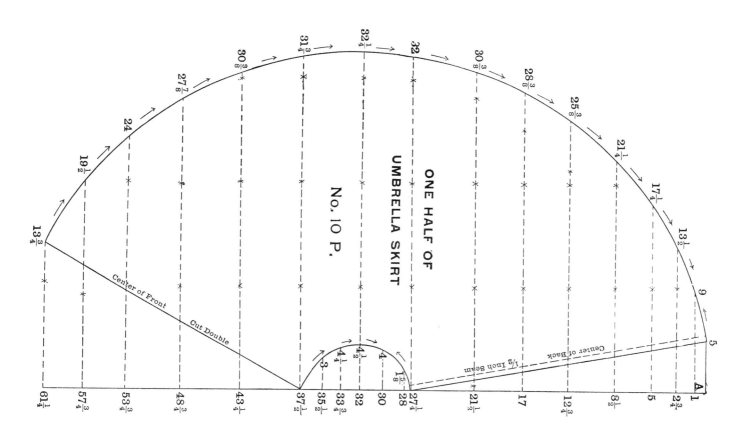

CHILD'S STREET COSTUME.

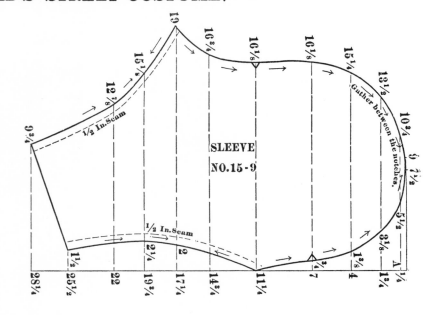

SLEEVE
NO. 15-9

Use the scale corresponding with the bust measure to draft the waist and jacket.

The waist is given on page 108. It consists of front, back and sleeve. Close it in the back, trim with braid, gather or pleat the sleeve.

The jacket is given on page 109. It consists of front, back, side-back, under-arm-gore, collar and facing, and collar lining, and two sleeve portions. Join the collar to the front according to the stars, notches and rings. Gather or pleat the sleeve between notches, use the umbrella skirt given on page 107. Draft by the waist measure, trim with braiding to correspond with the waist.

Regulate the length by the tape measure.

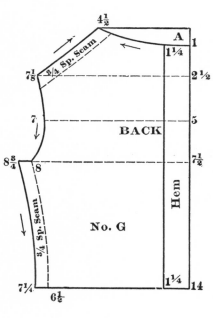

BACK

No. G

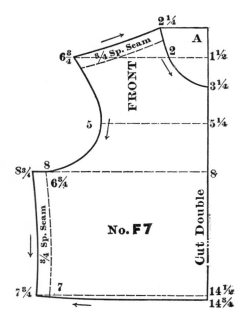

FRONT

No. F7

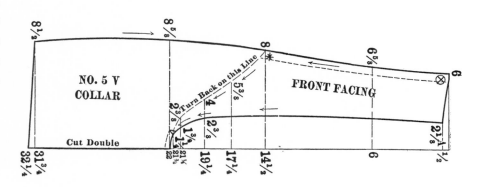

NO. 5 V
COLLAR

FRONT FACING

CHILD'S STREET COSTUME—Continued.

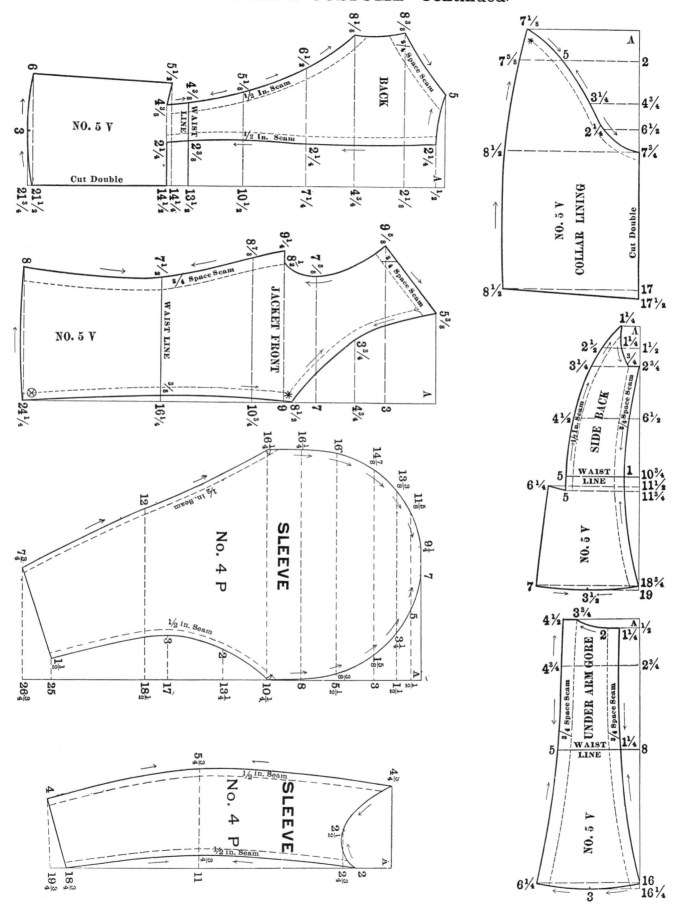

LADIES' STREET COSTUME.

Use the scale corresponding with the bust measure to draft the entire waist and sleeves, which consist of front, back, and side-back for the lining, and front, back, collar and three sleeve portions for the blouse.

Shir on the dotted lines, or as many times as desirable, and tack each shirring to the lining, allowing it to puff a little. Silk is very pretty made up in this way, or any soft material. The bottom may be hemmed and worn under the skirt. Close down the front invisibly with hooks and eyes.

The sleeves are given on page 112. Lay pleats, or gather between notches and sew to lining. It may be pleated in various ways, either double or single box pleats, or side pleats, meeting in the center.

The cape is given on page 112, is drafted by the bust measure. Line with silk or satin. Make of any suitable material. Regulate the length to suit. The neck may be finished in various ways, either with a stock collar and rosettes, or pleated lace with a bow in front, or a medici collar.

The skirt is given on page 113; is drafted by the waist measure. Is in three pieces, front, back, and side-gore. This is fitted without darts. Gather the front and side-gore enough to prevent drawing up. Gather or pleat the back breadth. Line throughout and face up the bottom with hair cloth. Bind the bottom with velvet. Trim with velvet or silk, or any other suitable material.

Regulate the length by the tape measure.

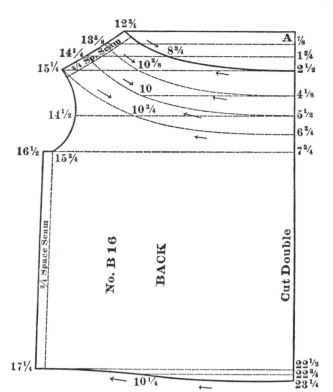

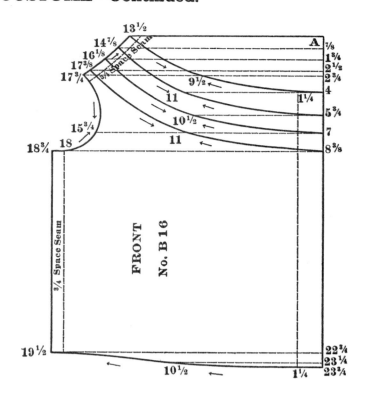

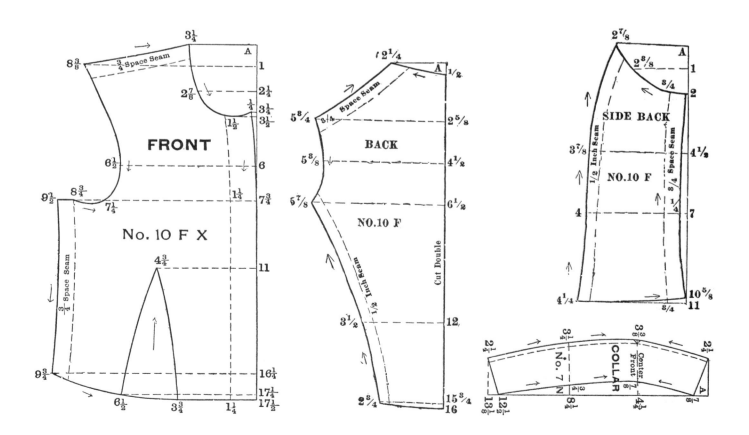

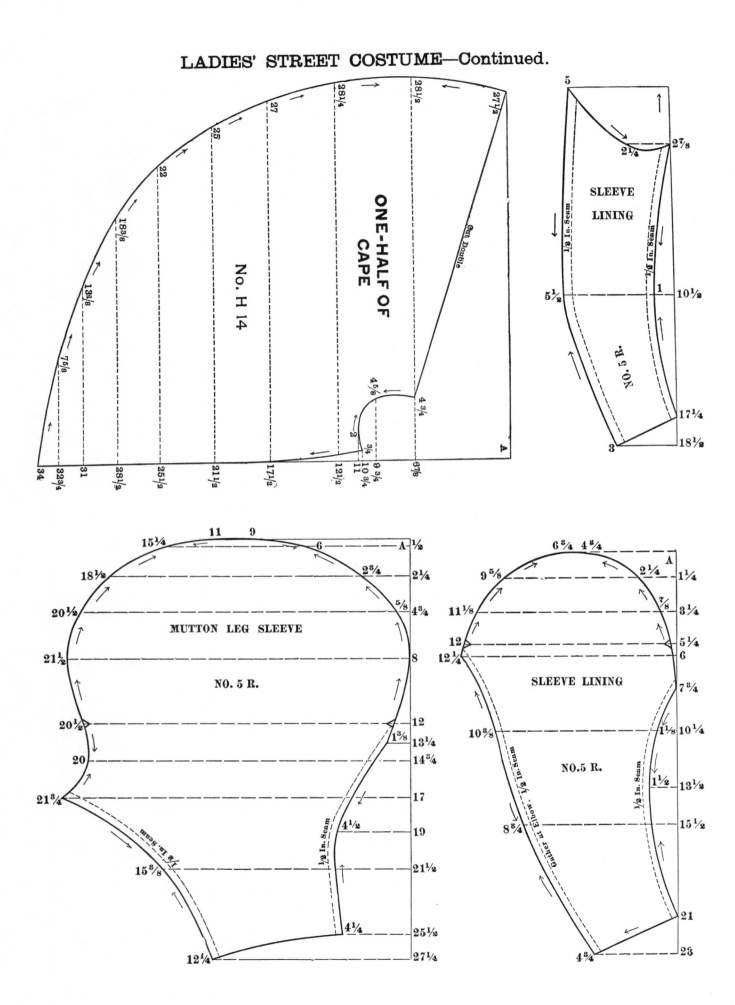

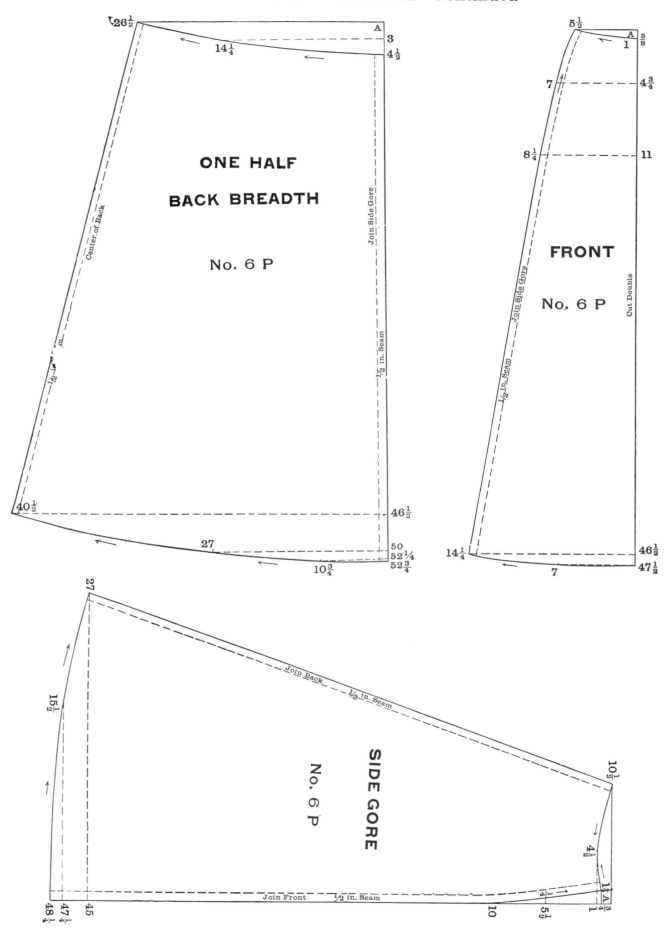

ONE HALF
BACK BREADTH

No. 6 P

FRONT

No. 6 P

SIDE GORE

No. 6 P

LADIES' STREET COSTUME.

Use the scale corresponding with the bust measure to draft the entire waist, which consists of front, back, two under-arm-gores, and three sleeve portions for the basque. This gives the plain, round effect in the back, and pointed in the front.

Fit very snugly, and bone each seam. Close in front invisibly with hooks and eyes. Any desirable decoration may be used.

The sleeves are given on page 116. Interline the puff with Tarletan, and gather, or pleat and sew to the tight sleeve on the dotted line.

The cape is given on page 115. Draft by bust measure. It consists of two yoke portions and ruffle. Make of lace and insertion, or fancy silk. We have omitted the skirt for want of room. Use any one given in this issue.

LADIES' STREET COSTUME—Continued.

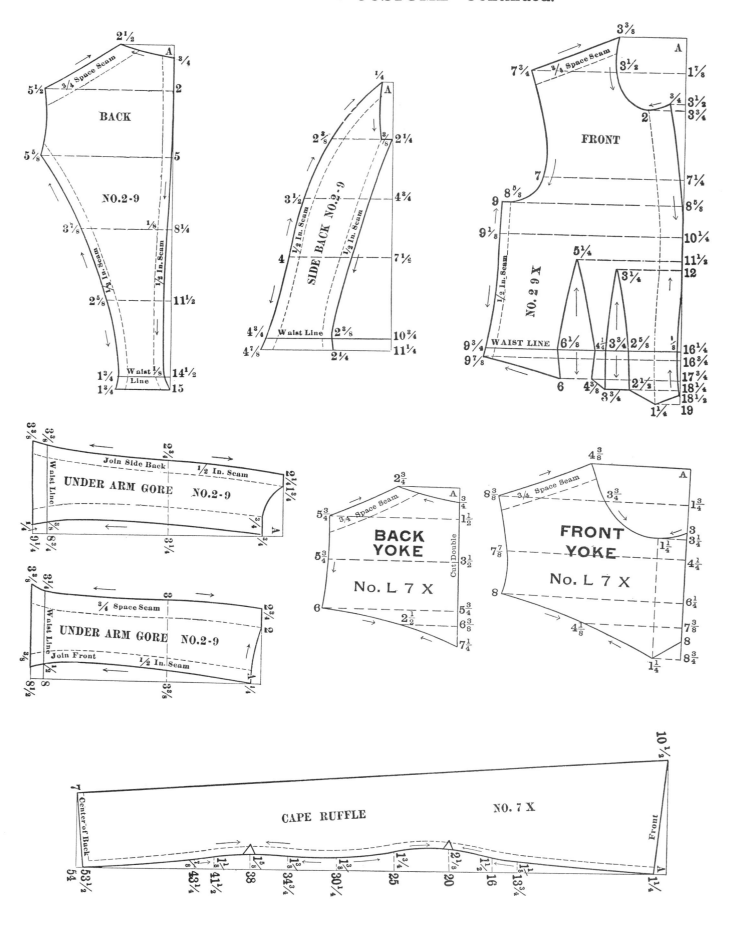

LADIES' STREET COSTUME—Continued.

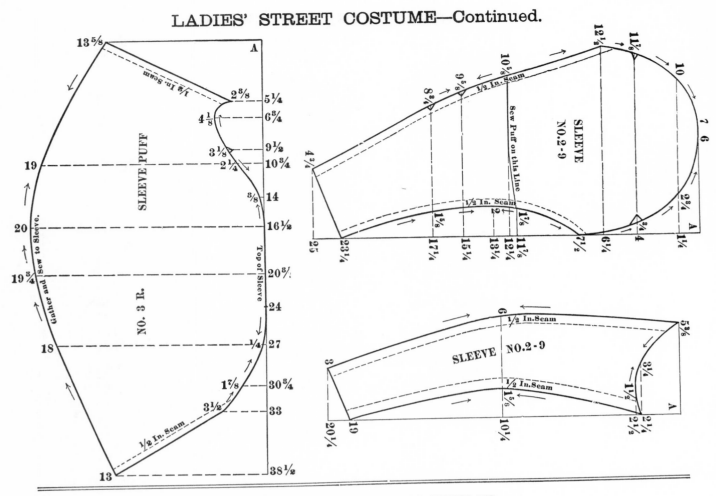

CHILD'S EMPIRE COSTUME.

Use the scale corresponding with the bust measure to draft the dress, which consists of two yoke pieces, and front and back skirt portions and the sleeve. Gather the skirt and sew to the yoke. Finish yoke with a ruffle of embroidery.

The sun bonnet is in five pieces.

Put two thicknesses of canvas on the front piece, and stitch many times so it will retain stiffness when laundered. Put the different parts together according to the notches, stars and rings. Make of any suitable material.

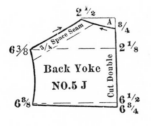

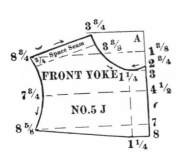

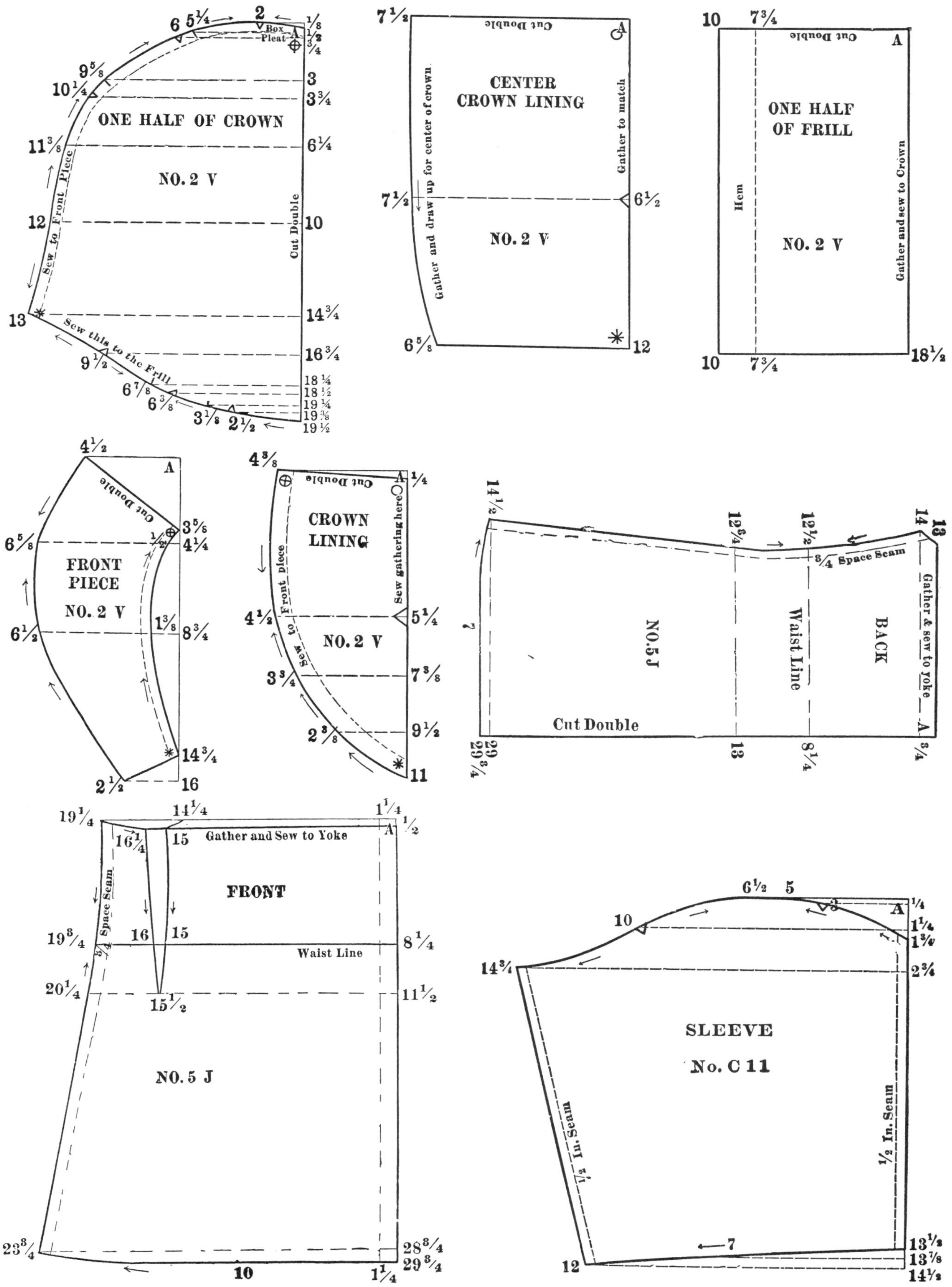

ONE HALF OF CROWN

NO. 2 V

Cut Double

Box Pleat

Sew to Front Piece

Sew this to the Frill

6 5¼ 2 ⅛ ⅛ ½ ¾
9⅝ 3 3¾ 6¼ 10 14¾ 16¾ 18¼ 18½ 19¼ 19⅜ 19½
10¼ 11⅜ 12 13 9½ 6⅞ 6⅜ 3⅛ 2½

CENTER CROWN LINING

NO. 2 V

Cut Double

Gather and draw up for center of crown

Gather to match

7½ 7½ 6½ 6⅝ 12

ONE HALF OF FRILL

NO. 2 V

Cut Double

Hem

Gather and sew to Crown

A
10 7¾ 10 7¾ 18½

FRONT PIECE

NO. 2 V

Cut Double

4½ A 3⅝ 4¼ 1⅜
6⅝ 6½ 8¾ 14¾ 16 2½

CROWN LINING

NO. 2 V

Cut Double

Sew to Front piece

Sew gathering here

4⅜ A ¼ 5¼ 7⅜ 9½ 11
4½ 3¾ 2⅜

BACK

NO. 5 J

Cut Double

Waist Line

Space Seam

Gather & sew to Yoke

14½ 12¾ 12½ 14 13 ⅞ 7 29 29¾ 13 8¼ 3¼

FRONT

NO. 5 J

Waist Line

Space Seam

Gather and Sew to Yoke

19¼ 14¼ 1¼ ½ 16¼ 15 A 19⅜ 16 15 8¼ 20¼ 15½ 11½ 23¾ 28¾ 29¾ 10 1¼

SLEEVE

No. C 11

½ In. Seam

½ In. Seam

6½ 5 A ¼ 1¼ 1⅜ 2¾ 10 14¾ 12 7 13½ 13⅛ 14½

CHILD'S COSTUME.

Use the scale corresponding with the bust measure to draft the entire waist and sleeves.

This gives the blouse effect. Lay pleats in front according to the notches. The 10-J front and back are for the under waist or lining.

Gather the sleeve puff and sew to the sleeve lining on curved line.

Draft the skirt by the waist measure. Lay the pleats according to the notches, and sew to the waist. Finish with white braid.

Regulate the length by the tape measure.

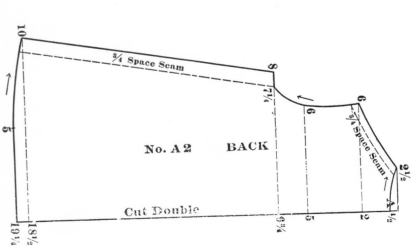

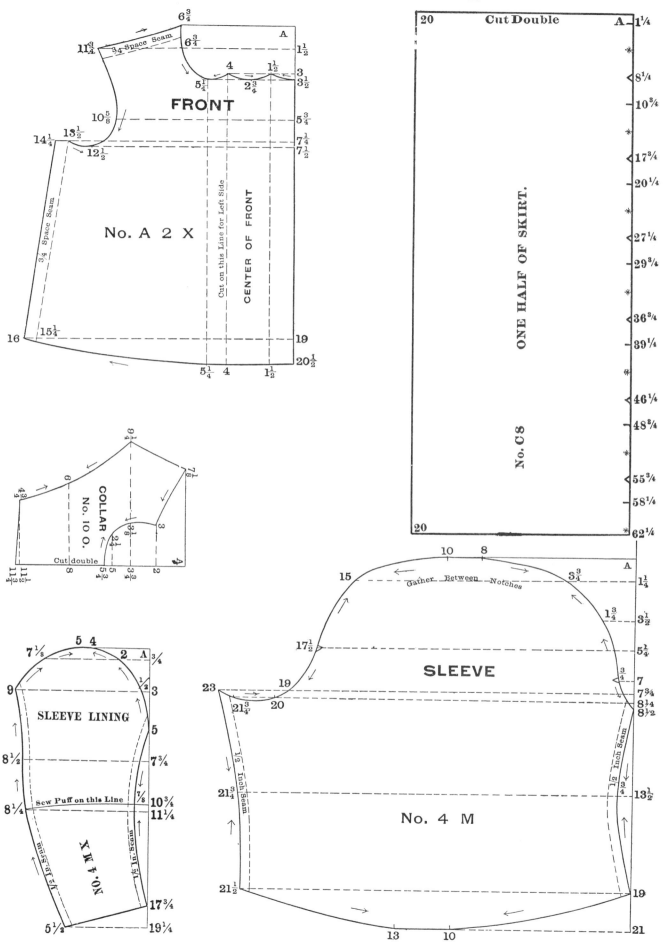

LADIES' TAILOR SUIT.

LADIES' TAILOR SUIT.

Use the scale corresponding with the bust measure to draft the entire Waist and Sleeves.

The Jacket is given on pages 121 and 122; consists of Front, Back, Side-back, Under-arm Gore, Rolling Collar and two Sleeve portions.

This is drafted in the usual way. It may be used as a Jacket or a Waist; if the latter, make a chemisette from the drafts given on page 122.

We have also given a plain pointed basque on pages 122 and 123.

Draft by the bust measure. Any style of decoration may be used, but stitching and buttons of every description are preferable.

The Skirt is given on pages 123 and 124. Draft by the waist measure, or any other skirt given in this issue. If a wider skirt is desired, add an extra side gore, lay the Back in pleats according to the notches. Regulate the length by the tape measure.

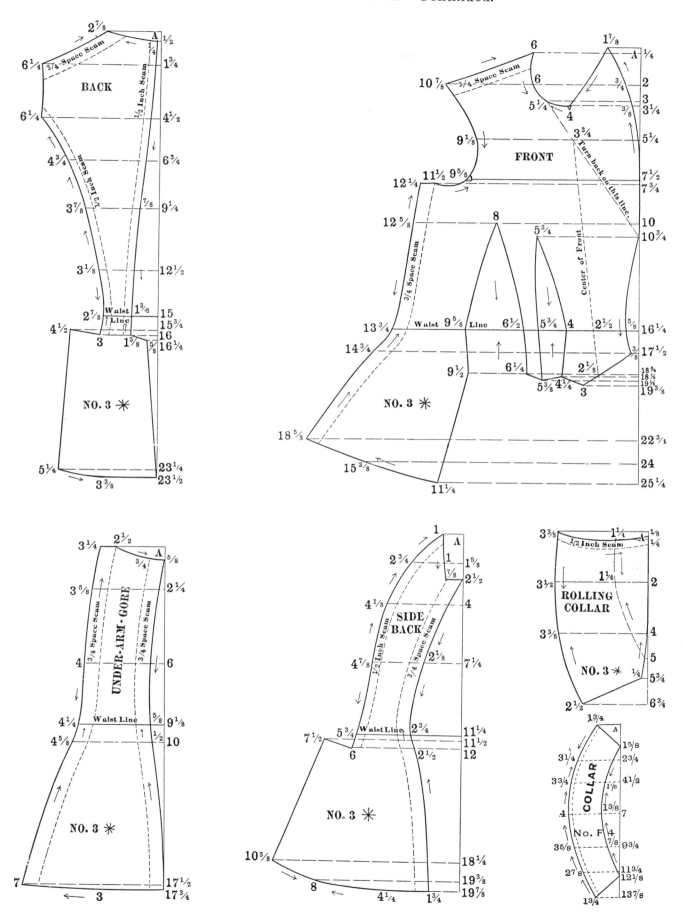

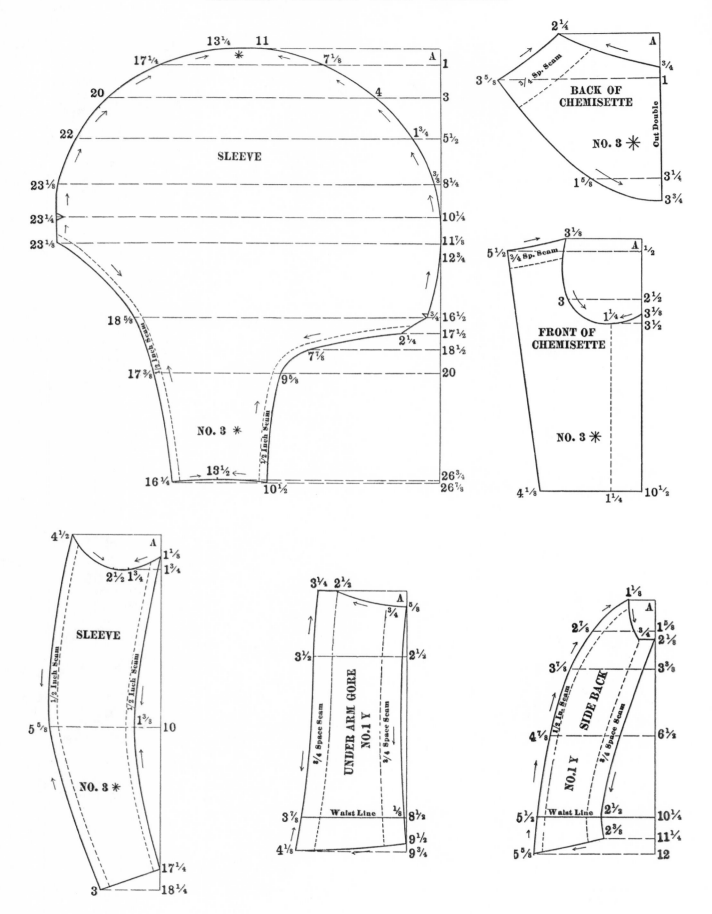

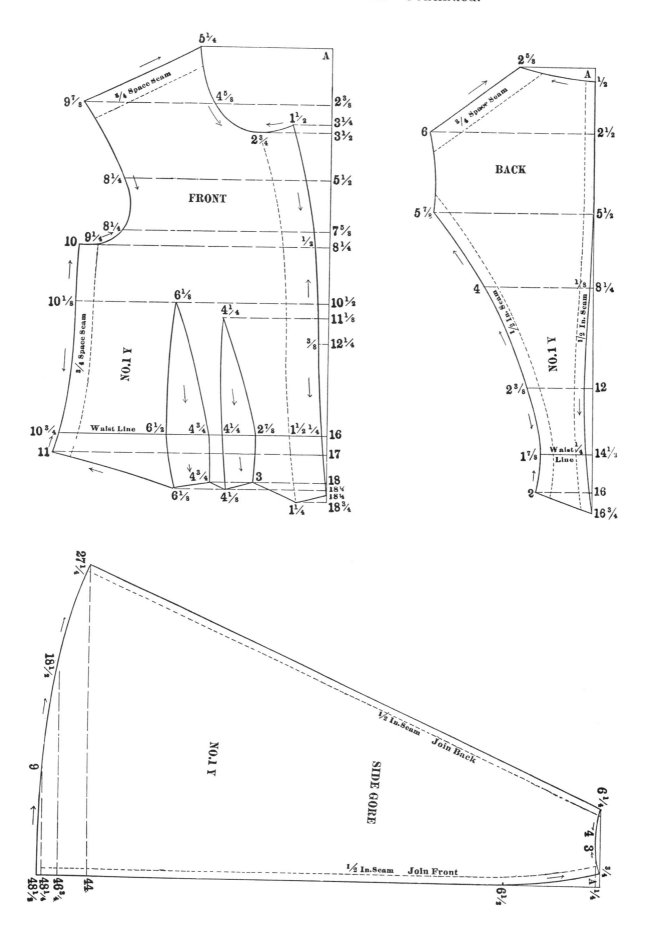

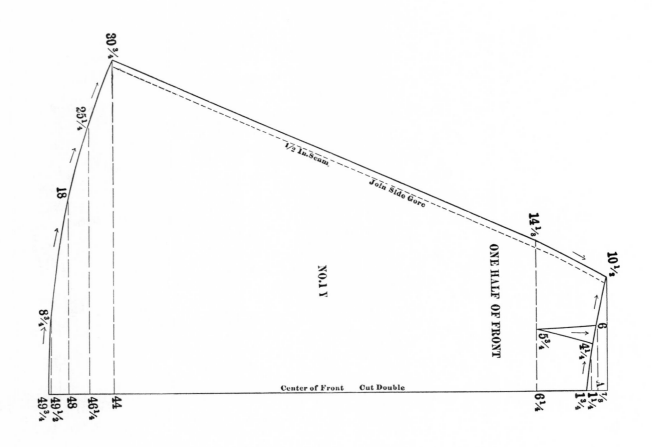

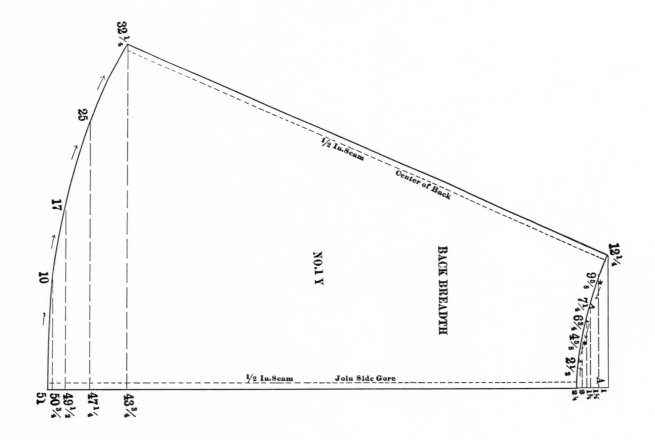

LADIES' STREET COSTUME.

LADIES' STREET COSTUME.

Use the scale corresponding with the Bust measure to draft the entire Waist, which consists of upper, under and center Fronts, Back, Collar, Cape and three Sleeve portions. Cut the lining from the Front, having one dart close down the Front with hooks and eyes. Cut the Center Front double, sew to the lining; sew the cape to the Upper Front and fasten securely to the lining on the right side and close with hooks and eyes on the left side. Trim the Cape, Sleeves and Skirt with fur. The Sleeves are given on Page 127. Gather the upper portion between the notches and sew to the lining. The Skirt is given on Pages 127 and 128. This is drafted by the Waist measure; it consists of Front, Back and two Side Gores. This may be finished off the same as the other Skirts we have described. Trim with fur or any other suitable trimming. Regulate the length by the tape measure.

LADIES' STREET COSTUME—Continued.

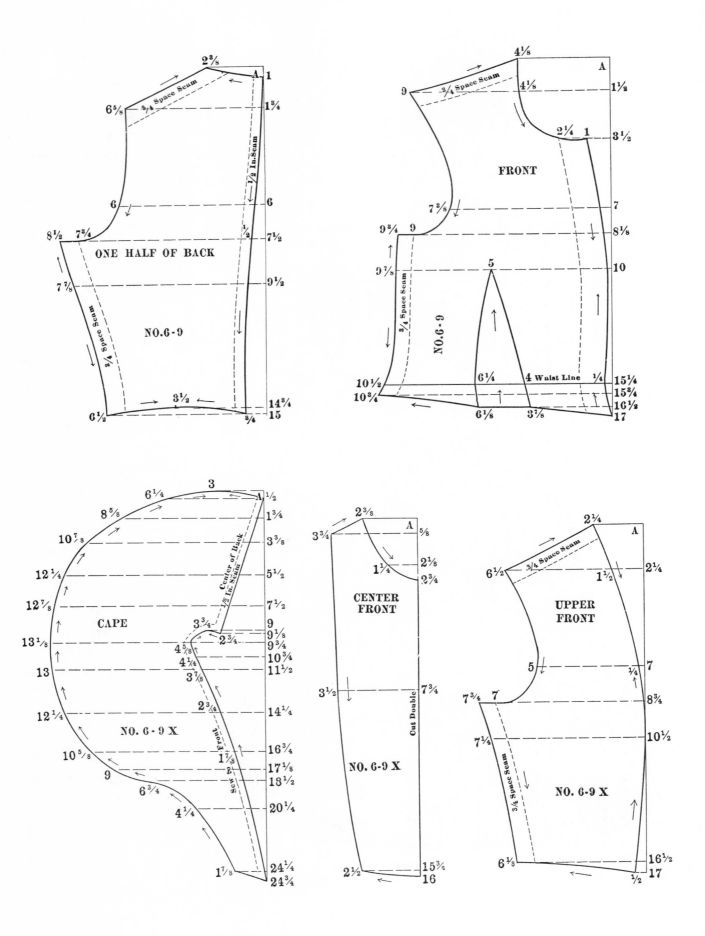

LADIES' STREET COSTUME—Continued.

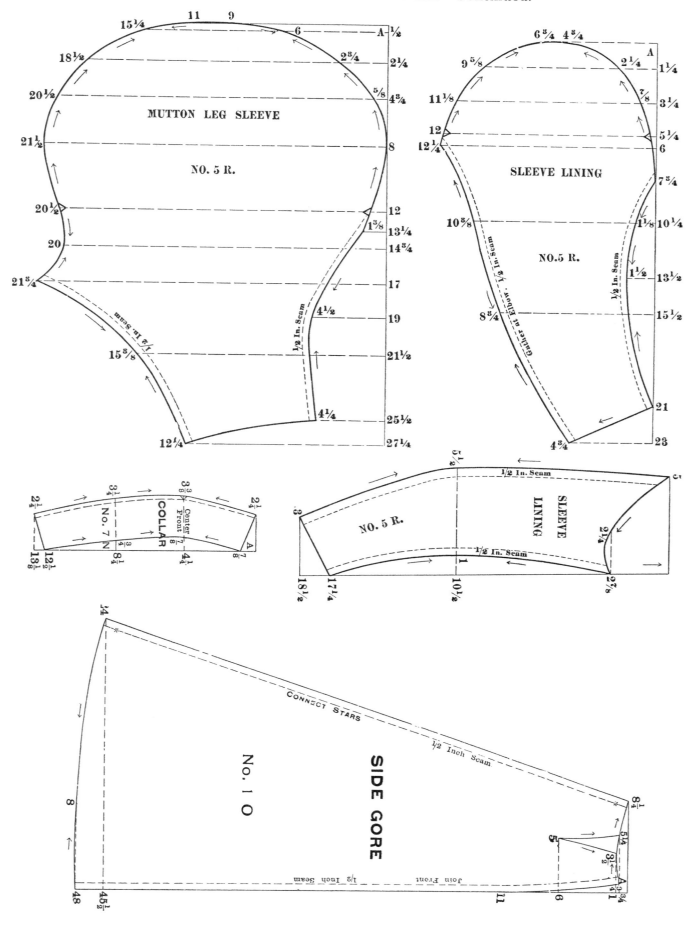

LADIES' STREET COSTUME—Continued.

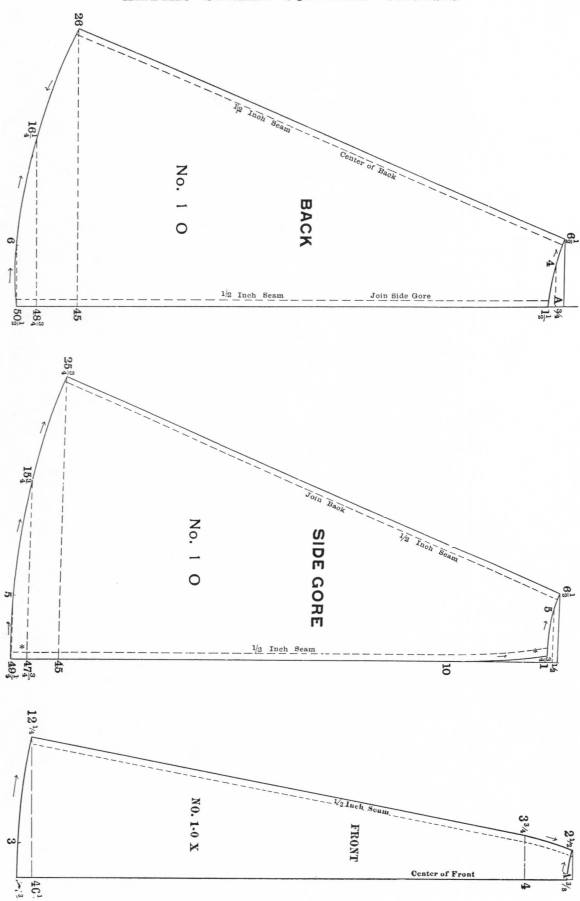

LADIES' COSTUME.

Use the scale corresponding with the bust measure to draft the entire Waist and Cape.

The Waist consists of two Fronts, Back, Side-back, Under-arm Gore, Collar, Full Front and three Sleeve Portions. This gives the Round Back and slightly Pointed Front. Cut the lining only from the draft having two darts. Lay pleats in the Upper Front according to the notches; close invisibly with hooks and eyes.

The Bishop Sleeve, given on page 131, is in three pieces, two Linings and a Puff. Line the Puff with sea-grass or fibre chamois; gather the bottom and sew to the sleeve lining on the dotted lines to form a cuff. This is especially suitable for tall ladies, as it tends to diminish the height and broaden the figure.

The Cape is given on page 132, and the Rolling Collar on page 131. This may be made of any material. If it is to be made of very heavy cloth, draw a line from the neck, or figure 18⅝, down to 4¼ on bottom cross-line and cut this away. Interline with tarlatan, sea-grass or fibre chamois. Regulate the length by the tape measure.

Draft the Under-waist by the scale corresponding with the bust measure. It is suitable for an under-waist or corset-cover. Close in front with buttons and button-holes.

LADIES' COSTUME—Continued.

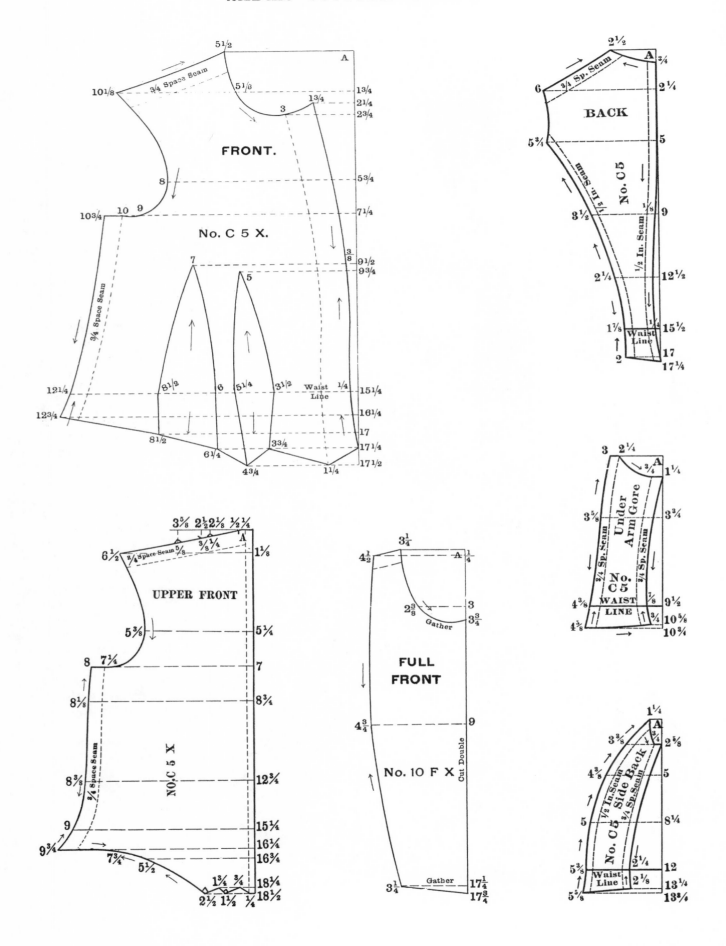

LADIES' BISHOP SLEEVE.

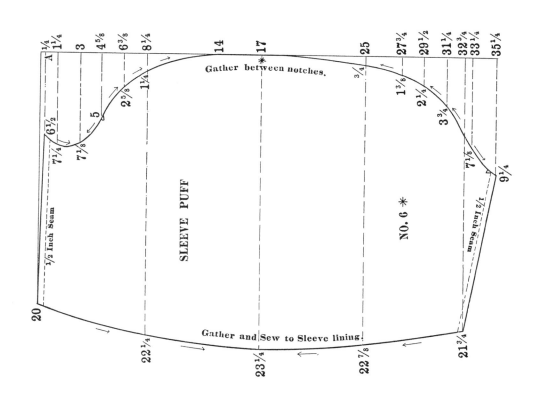

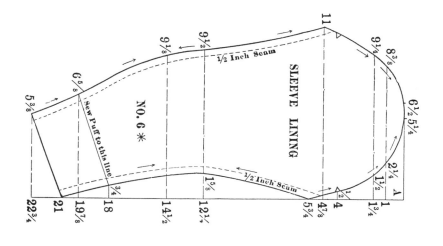

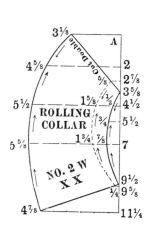

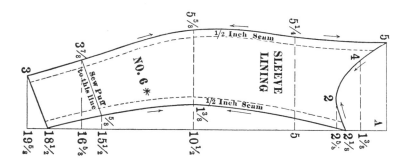

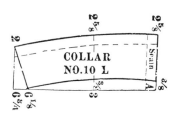

LADIES' CAPE.

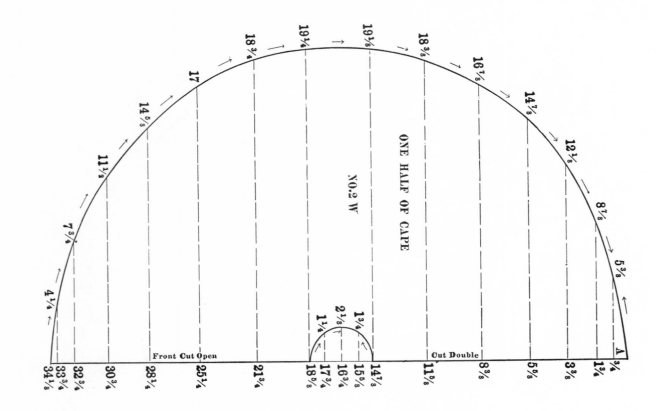

ONE HALF OF CAPE

NO.2 W

Front Cut Open

Cut Double

LADIES' UNDERWAIST.

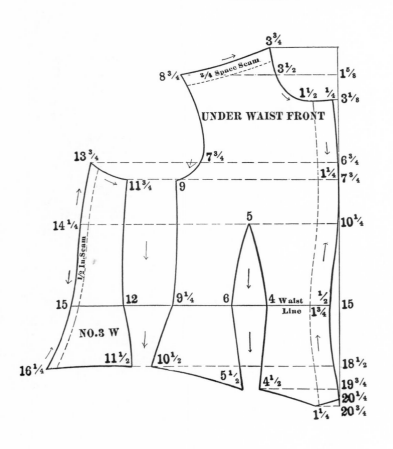

UNDER WAIST FRONT

NO.3 W

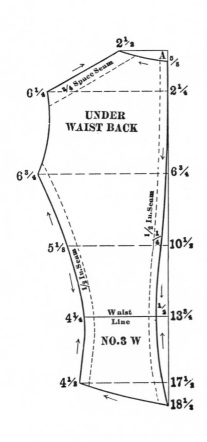

UNDER WAIST BACK

NO.3 W

MISSES' COSTUME.

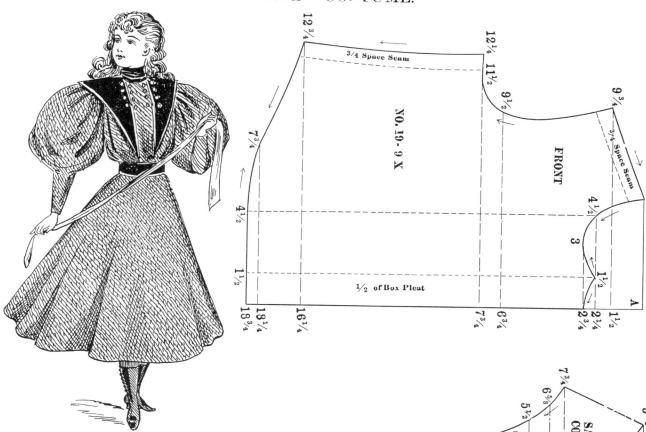

MISSES' COSTUME.

Use the scale corresponding with the bust measure to draft the entire Waist and Sleeve. Cut the Front lining only from the draft having one dart. Lay a box pleat down the center of upper Front, carry the Sailor Collar down the Front under the box pleat, finish with small gold or pearl buttons, close in the back invisibly. Gather the Sleeve between notches.

The Skirt is given on pages 134 and and 135. Draft by waist measure. Is in two pieces, Front and Back. There may be two, three or four pleats for the Back. Regulate the length by the tape line.

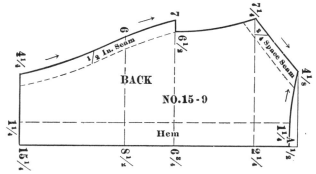

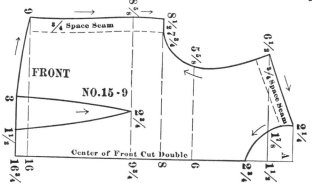

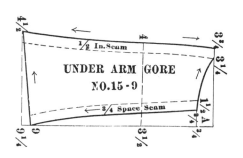

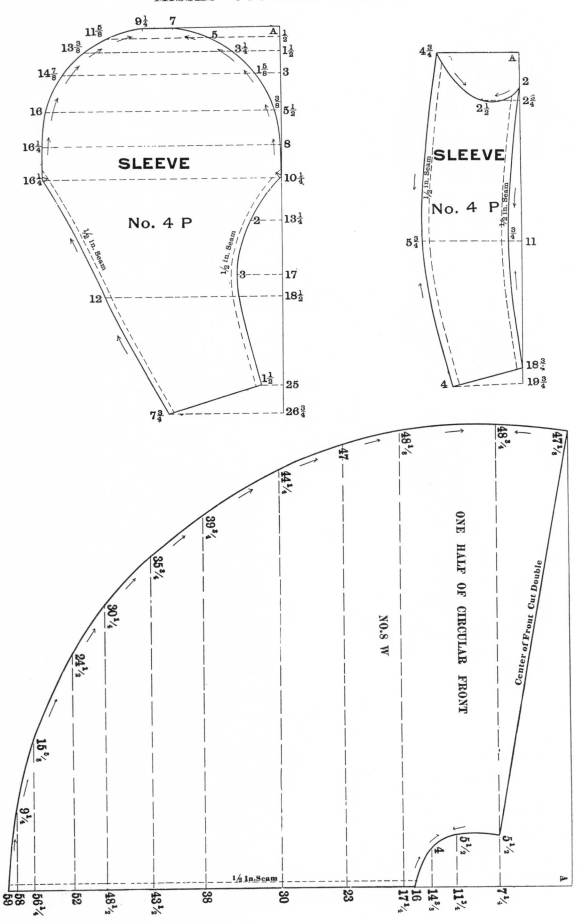

SLEEVE

No. 4 P

SLEEVE

No. 4 P

ONE HALF OF CIRCULAR FRONT

NO. 8 W

Center of Front Cut Double

MISSES' COSTUME—Continued.

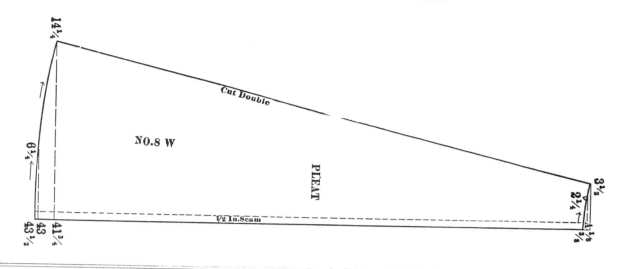

NO.8 W

Cut Double

PLEAT

14¼

6¼

43½
43
41¾

½ In.Seam

3½
2¼
1⅛
⅜

CHILD'S COSTUME.

CHILD'S COSTUME.

Use the scale corresponding with the bust measure to draft the entire Jacket, which consists of Front, Back, Collar and three Sleeve Portions.

This is a Box Jacket. Cut the Back double; the Front is double-breasted; the Sleeves are in the Bishop style; gather the puff and sew to the linings on the dotted line. The lower part is for the cuff. Use any Child's Skirt and Waist. We have omitted them for want of room.

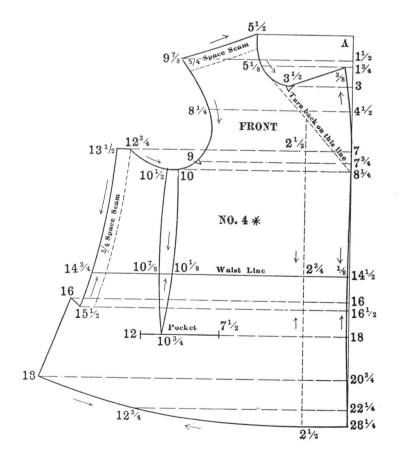

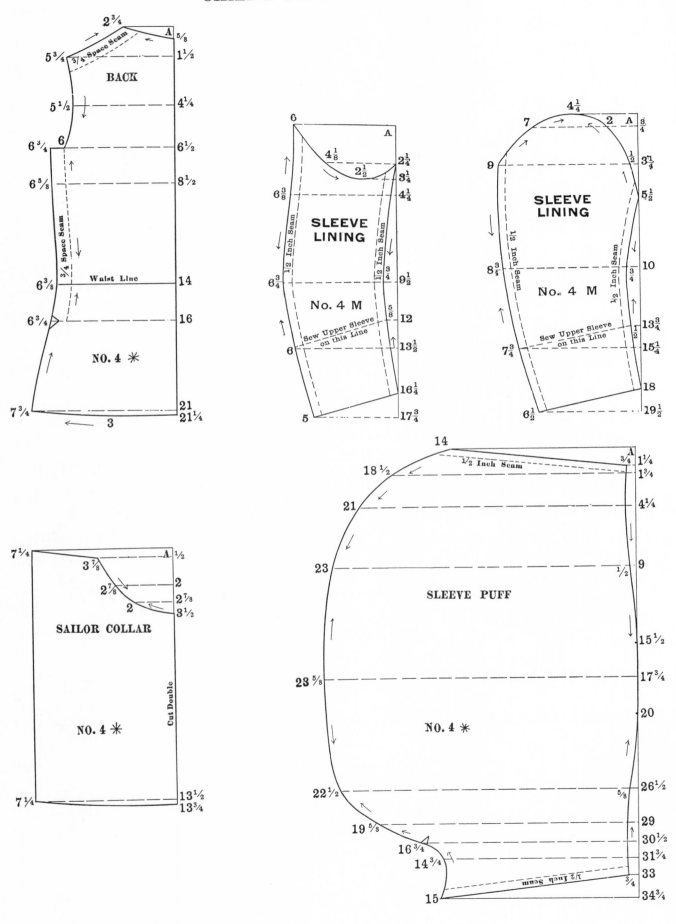

CHILD'S LONG CLOAK.

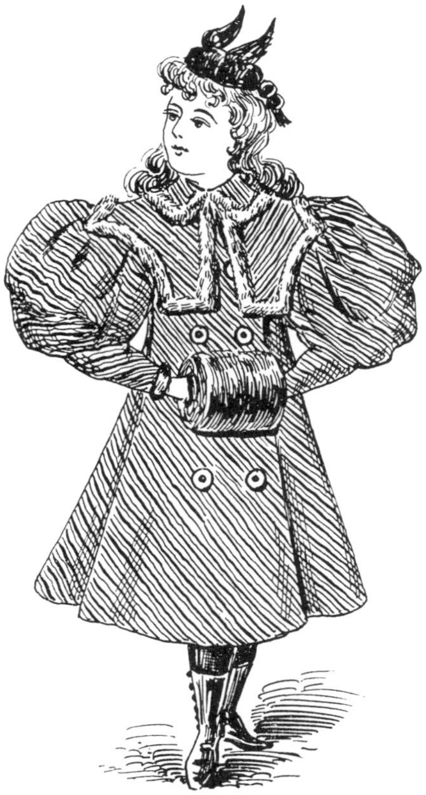

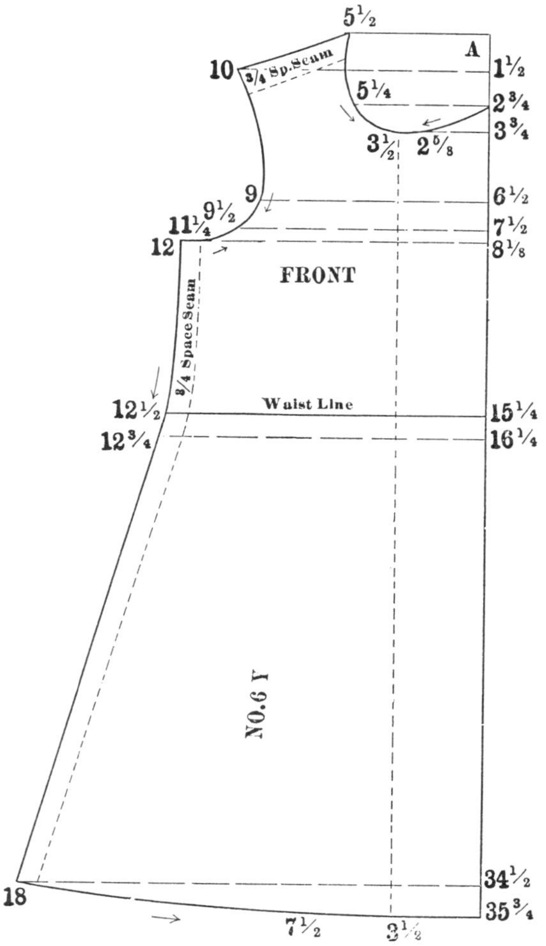

5½
A
10
3/4 Sp. Seam
1½
5¼
2¾
3¾
3½
2⅝
9
6½
11¼
9½
7½
12
8⅛
FRONT
3/4 Space Seam
12½
Waist Line
15¼
12¾
16¼
NO.6 Y
34½
18
35¾
7½
3½

CHILD'S LONG CLOAK.

Use the scale corresponding with the bust measure to draft the entire garment, which consists of Front, Back, Side-back, Under-arm Gore, Collar, Cape and Sleeves.

This has been inserted by special request. Is suitable for a School Cloak. Make of any heavy material. Trim the Cape with fur or astrakhan. Make it as long as the dress skirt. Regulate the length by the tape measure.

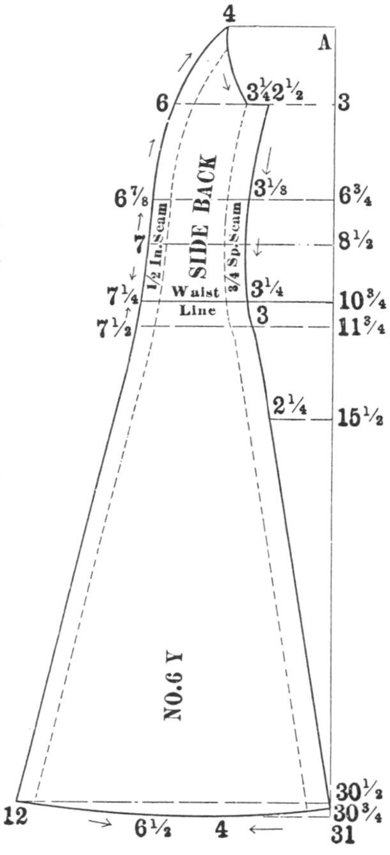

4
A
6
3¼
2½
3
SIDE BACK
6⅞
3⅛
6¾
1/2 In. Seam
3/4 Sp. Seam
7
8½
7¼
Waist Line
3¼
10¾
7½
3
11¾
2¼
15½
NO.6 Y
30½
12
30¾
6½
4
31

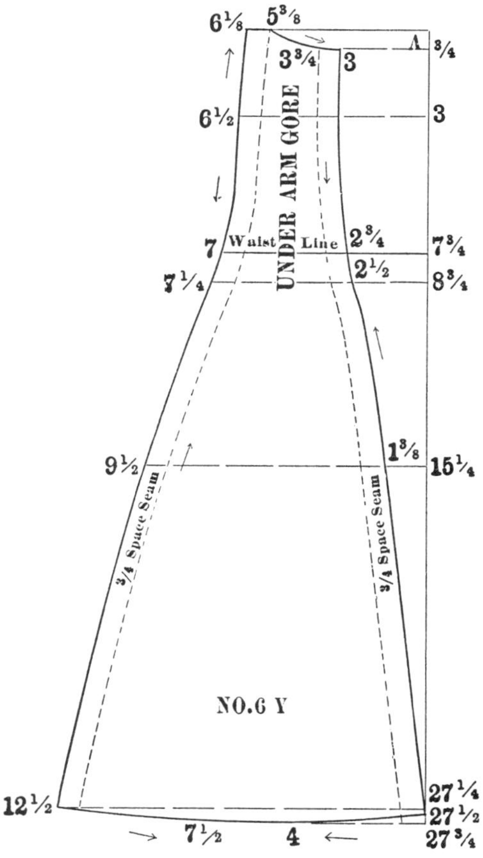

6⅛
5⅜
A
¾
3¾
3
6½
3
UNDER ARM GORE
7
Waist Line
2¾
7¾
7¼
2½
8¾
9½
1⅜
15¼
3/4 Space Seam
3/4 Space Seam
NO.6 Y
27¼
12½
27½
7½
4
27¾

CHILD'S LONG CLOAK.

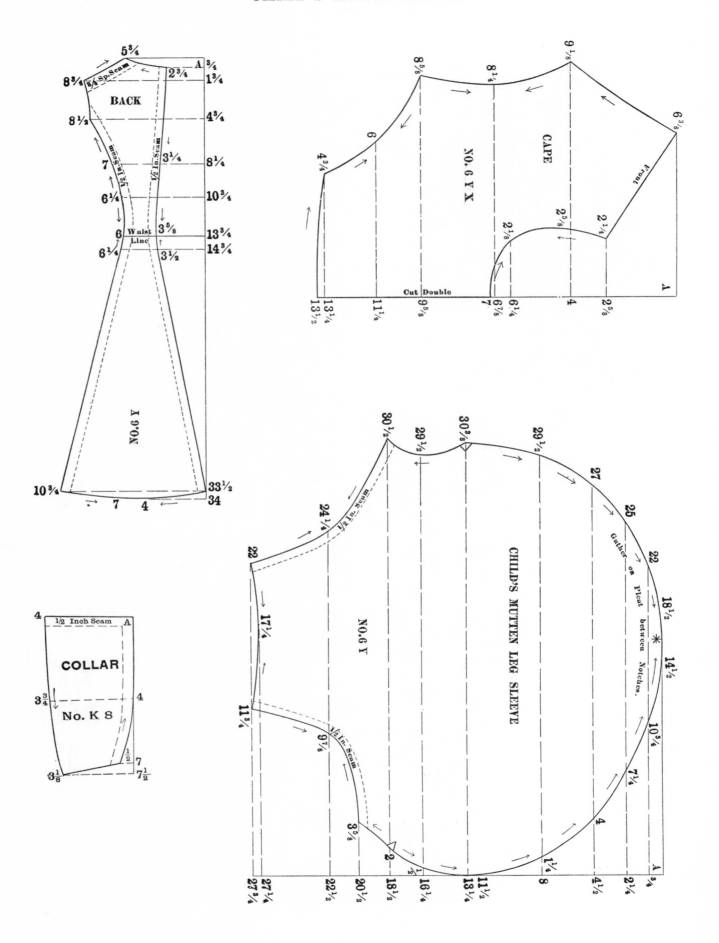

MISSES' COSTUME.

MISSES' COSTUME.

Use the scale corresponding with the bust measure to draft the entire waist and sleeves, which consists of two Fronts, Back and two Sleeve portions. Turn the upper front down on the dotted line close on the left side; finish with a rosette or bow of ribbon. Draft the skirt by the waist measure. Regulate length by the tape measure.

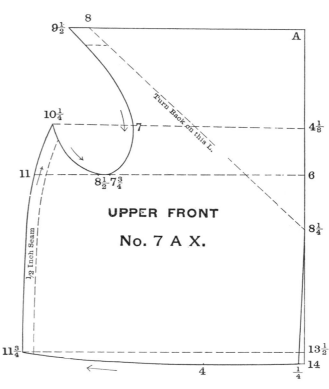

UPPER FRONT
No. 7 A X.

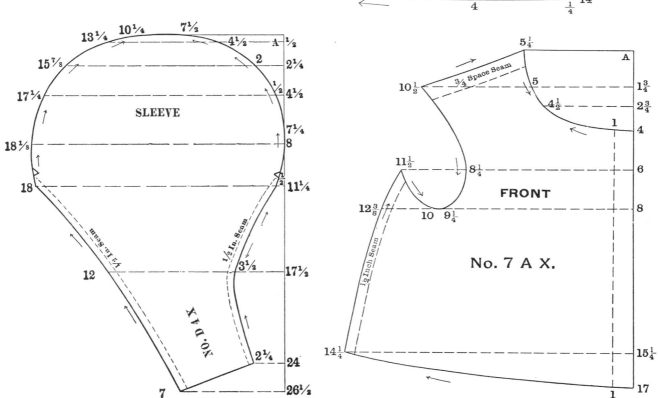

SLEEVE

NO. D 4 X.

FRONT

No. 7 A X.

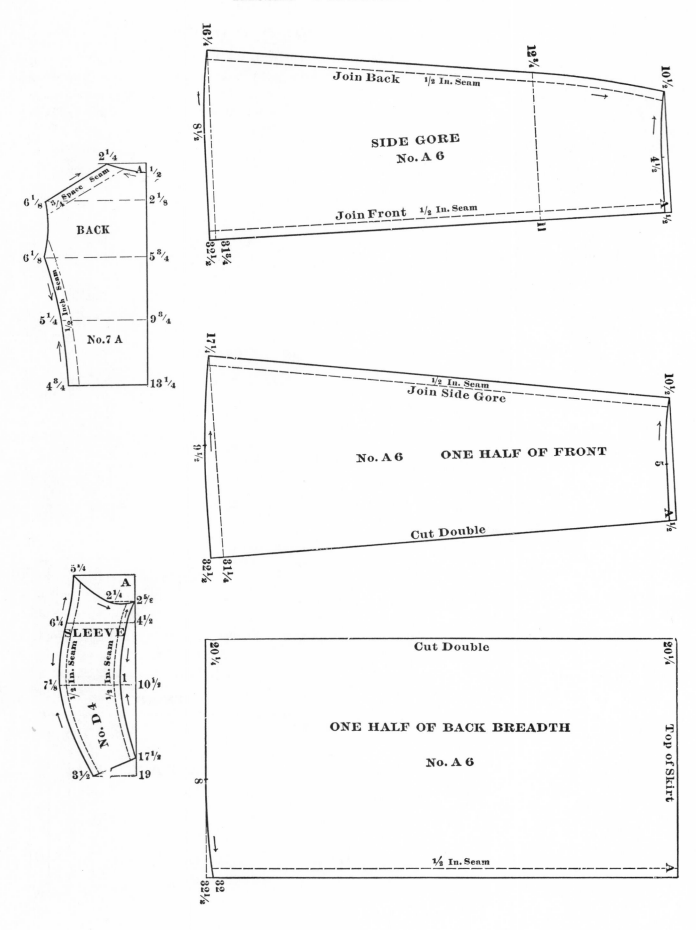